CHRISTOPHER MARLOWE

The Tragicall Hiftoy of the Life and Death

of Doctor Fauftus.

With new Additions.

Written by *Ch. Mar.*

LONDON,
Printed for *Iohn Wright*, and are to be fold at his fhop without
Newgate, at the figne of the Bible. 1620.

CHRISTOPHER
MARLOWE

by

PHILIP HENDERSON

Second Edition

BARNES & NOBLE

BOOKS
10 East 53d St., New York 10022
(a division of Harper & Row Publishers, Inc.)

Published in the U.S.A. 1974
by
HARPER & ROW PUBLISHERS, INC.
BARNES AND NOBLE IMPORT DIVISION

Christopher Marlowe
first published in 1952
by Longmans, Green and Co., London
This edition first published in 1974
by The Harvester Press Limited, Brighton

'Christopher Marlowe' © Philip Henderson
1952, 1974

ISBN 06 492811 X
75-306225

Typesetting by Campbell Graphics Ltd.,
Newcastle upon Tyne
Printed in Great Britain by Redwood Press Limited
Trowbridge, Wiltshire
Bound by Cedric Chivers Limited
Portway, Bath

ACKNOWLEDGEMENTS

My indebtedness to all those who have studied Christopher Marlowe is so general that I may not have acknowledged it in every instance; but references will be found to those works I have drawn upon principally. It is enough to say that the present book could not have been written but for the previous labours of such scholars as: Dr. F. S. Boas, Mr. Leslie Hotson, Dr. Mark Eccles, Mr. John Bakeless, Professor Una Ellis-Fermor, Miss M. C. Bradbrook and Sir Walter Greg. I am also indebted to the recent work of Dr. H. P. Kocher, which, taken in conjunction with Professor Ellis-Fermor's inspiring book and the brief investigation into the psychological roots of his genius carried out by Dr. Mario Praz, gives what is perhaps the most convincing and consistent estimate of Marlowe yet attempted. Dr. Boas's pioneer work on the career of the spy Robert Poley has thrown much light on a side of Marlowe's life which has been until comparatively recently no more than a matter of conjecture. Stimulating, too, I have found Wyndham Lewis's study of the influence of Machiavelli and the Italian Renaissance on the Elizabethan dramatists in his book *The Lion and the Fox*.

I am particularly grateful to my friends Christopher Gillie and Eirian James for reading my manuscript and for much valuable criticism.

P.H.

CONTENTS

ILLUSTRATIONS

The quotations from Marlowe's plays and poems are
taken from Professor Tucker Brooke's edition, the
spelling of which has been modernized for the con-
venience of the general reader, though the Elizabethan
punctuation has been retained, as it is essential to the
rhythmic pointing of the verse.

NEW INTRODUCTION

As a glance at the Bibliography will show, the volume of critical and biographical studies of Marlowe since this book first appeared in 1952 has been considerable. But this has only gone to show that scholarly opinion of both the plays and of the man himself is sharply divided. Christopher Marlowe remains something of an enigma, as ambiguous in himself as in the tone of his writings. Even the portrait discovered at Corpus Christi College, Cambridge, cannot definitely be taken as an authentic likeness, while its striking similarity to the Grafton portrait of 'Shakespeare' still further complicates the issue.[1] We do not know enough to form a complete picture of the man, though we know just enough to give rise to conjecture, much of it contradictory.

A short review of the established facts about Marlowe himself may, therefore, be helpful. We at least have his signature as 'Christopher Marley'—a common variation of his name—as witness to the will of one Katherine Benchkyn of Canterbury, discovered in 1939 by F.W. Tyler. This tallies with the manuscript page of a scene from *The Massacre at Paris* known as the Collier Leaf.[2] Thanks to the

[1] A.D. Wraight & V.F. Stern, *In Search of Christopher Marlowe, 1965.*
[2] Ibid.

exhaustive researches of Dr. William Urry, Cathedral
and City Archivist, we know a good deal about
Marlowe's turbulent family.[1] We know now that his
mother was a Dover girl and not the daughter of the
Rev. Christopher Arthur, as formerly supposed. Dr.
Urry also discovered that in 1592, about seven
months before he was killed at Deptford, Marlowe
was engaged in a fight with William Corkine, musician
and tailor, near the Chequers Inn, Canterbury. This
was evidently not a very serious affray, however, for
after the hearing the two young men left the court
arm in arm. In May of the same year two Shoreditch
constables complained that 'they went in fear of their
lives' because of him, and on 9 May Marlowe
appeared before Sir Owen Hopton and was bound
over in £20 to appear at the Michaelmas Assizes. On
the basis of a letter from the Privy Council to
Cambridge University, Professor Leslie Hotson
deduced that the 'Christopher Morley' there
mentioned was engaged in secret service work as early
as 1587, while still at the University. On 18
September, 1589, Marlowe was engaged in another
duel, this time in the Shoreditch theatrical district
with William Bradley, the son of a Holborn publican
and a well-known roisterer.[2] But Bradley's quarrel
was with Thomas Watson, and on his appearance
Bradley set about him. The result was Bradley's

[1] 'Marlowe and Canterbury', *Times Literary Supplement,* February
13, 1964. Dr. Urry describes Marlowe's father as "a noisy, self-assertive,
improvident fellow". His sister Ann was described by a contemporary
as a 'malicious, uncharitable person seeking the unjust vexation of her
neighbours ... a scold, common swearer and blasphemer of the name
of God'.

[2] Mark Eccles, *Christopher Marlowe in London,* Cambridge, Mass.,
1934.

death. Marlowe and Watson were arrested and lodged in Newgate gaol. But when he appeared before Sir Roger Manwood, who had an estate near Canterbury, Marlowe was discharged with a warning to keep the peace. On Manwood's death he wrote his epitaph.

At the end of May 1593 Marlowe met his own death in a small room at Eleanor Bull's house on Deptford Strand, where he had been spending the day with three friends, all of whom had connections with the Secret Service. The inquisition of the inquest has recently been re-examined by Mr. Gavin Thurston, H.M. Coroner, County of London (Western District). Though many scholars have regarded the evidence given there by Ingram Frizer and others as highly suspect, Mr. Thurston remarks that the nature of the wound inflicted on Marlowe as a cause of death 'is so wildly improbable that it alone sets the seal of authenticity on the inquest' and that all things considered, the very oddity of Frizer's evidence is the best argument for its truth.[1] 'There is nothing to suggest that the inquisition was not regularly executed', Mr. Thurston concludes, 'and the probable mechanism of Marlowe's death was so unusual and unexpected that fabrication is unlikely.'

From the inquisition we learn that Marlowe was wounded 'over the right eye', which has always been taken to mean that Frizer's dagger pierced his skull, an impossibility in the circumstances of their struggle. As Mr. Thurston remarks: "over the right eye" does not give the precise position of the wound. However, if the blade entered the eye socket between the eyeball and eyebrow instantaneous death could

[1] 'Inquest—Christopher Marlowe's Death', *Contemporary Review*, March/April, 1964.

result. Such injuries are extremely rare but the proposition offers the only reasonable explanation of Marlowe's instant death.' On the question of evidence Mr. Thurston observes: 'In the sixteenth century witnesses at an inquest were examined orally and no depositions or notes of evidence were taken. The findings were then incorporated in the one inquisition document. It is probable that all those who were present in the house were questioned by the Coroner, including Mistress Bull, so that the facts set down are the most reliable possible record.' Such an authoritative statement is of the utmost importance in attempting to decide whether Marlowe was murdered or not, even though common sense suggests that no sixteenth century jury would have seen anything suspicious in such an ordinary occurrence as a 'tavern brawl'.

According to the evidence that emerged at the Deptford inquest, Marlowe suddenly attacked Frizer from behind, giving him a couple of cuts about the head. For this purpose he apparently borrowed Frizer's dagger, while the latter was sitting at a table playing backgammon with Poley and Skeres—an action which bears out Thomas Kyd's description of Marlowe in his letter to Sir John Puckering, as in the habit of 'attempting sudden privy injuries to men'. One need not waste much sympathy on Ingram Frizer, for although sitting, as he said he was, wedged between Poley and Skeres so that he could not get away from Marlowe in the struggle to get back his dagger, he nevertheless managed to stab it into Marlowe's eye. Probably he did not mean to kill him. We are told, however, that just before the attack Marlowe and Frizer 'were in speech and uttered one to the other divers malicious words for the reason that they could not be at one nor agree about the payment of the sum of pence, that is, *le recknyinge,* there . . .'—an almost homely detail which suddenly brings the whole thing vividly before us. Such a motive is quite sufficient to explain the origin of the quarrel without dragging in complicated political plots. Had the Council wished to get rid of Marlowe they could easily have done so without resorting to such a hole-in-the-corner method. As it was he had been ordered to report to them daily until such time as they were ready to question him.

The kind of man Marlowe was, one might think, is sufficiently evident from his plays, until we discover that each of his plays is quite different from the others and that *Hero and Leander* is different again. Indeed, many readers may well find themselves in the position of Professor L.C. Knights who said that, 'unless we have a very strong *parti pris,* we are likely to find ourselves veering with each fresh re-consideration of the major plays.'[1] In any case, how far are we justified in imputing to a dramatist the opinions and sentiments of his characters? Thus, while *Tamburlaine* is one long glorification of power mania, *Doctor Faustus,* in which the scholar's pretensions to world dominion through magic are treated ironically, might have been written by a devout Catholic. *The Massacre at Paris,* again, is the crudest patriotic Protestant propaganda and *The Jew of Malta* mocks at all forms of religion. 'A god is not so glorious as a King' we are told in *Tamburlaine:*

---

[1] 'The Strange Case of Christopher Marlowe', *Further Explorations,* 1965, pp.75–6.

but in *Edward the Second* the wretched king ends up in the castle sewer, before being murdered in a manner which is a savagely ironical comment on his homosexual proclivities. Homosexual feeling is again strong in *Hero and Leander,* in the rapturous description of Leander's body, but it is reduced to farce in the lines describing Leander's encounter with Neptune as he swims the Hellespont. And though Marlowe was credited by Richard Baines with saying that 'all they that love not tobacco and boys were fools'—which reads suspiciously like a phrase coined to shock his contemporaries, there is nothing more than hearsay on which to base Dr. Rowse's assertion that Marlowe was 'a well-known homosexual'[1] If he was really in the habit of saying half the things attributed to him by Baines and Kyd, one can only wonder how he managed to survive as long as he did. Rash and impulsive as he evidently was and fascinated by all forms of unorthodox speculation, what he actually *believed,* it seems to me, may be seen in *Doctor Faustus.*

It was the same mind that dramatised the outrageous and brutal scenes of *Tamburlaine* and *Edward the Second* as conceived the lyrically tender passages in *Hero and Leander,* with its acute understanding of feminine psychology and the endearing absurdities of adolescent love. But it is the fashion now to emphasise the ironical asides rather than the entrancing beauty of that poem as a whole. In fact, many commentators today spend their time discovering almost everything in Marlowe's poetry except its beauty, though it is true that the poems nearest in tone to *Hero and Leander* are Ovid's

[1] A.L. Rowse, *Christopher Marlowe: A Biography, 1964.*

Amores, which Marlowe had translated, and Byron's *Don Juan.* Thus while the more heady lyrical flights of *Tamburlaine* suggest a state of unresisted euphoria, their author was capable at the same time of a cool control, a detachment shown frequently by what appears to us as the tone of caricature which offsets Tamburlaine's most atrocious acts.

What finally emerges from the plays is an unusually complex and contradictory mind and temperament. Marlowe's supermen are not simply, in the words of J.A. Symonds, 'day-dreams of their maker's deep desires'. It was T.S. Eliot who first pointed out that Marlowe often achieves his finest effects by stopping just short of caricature, and it is precisely this subtle ambivalence of tone which makes him so fascinating in an uneasy age like our own.

It used to be said that Marlowe had no sense of humour. Nowadays there is a tendency to see comic touches everywhere in his work. Especially is this so in the papers presented at a recent symposium held at the University of York, where we read of the 'Comic Method in *Hero and Leander*' and 'Marlowe and the "Commic Distance" '.[1] But one of the most interesting developments of modern criticism is the importance given in this collection to *Dido, Queen of Carthage.* 'The power and depth of Dido's emotion,' writes Dr. Brian Gibbons, 'are dramatically realised in what we are accustomed to think of as an uniquely Shakespearean manner; and in fact it is essentially the *dramatic* power of *Dido* which influences Shakespeare in *Antony and Cleopatra.* In Shakespeare's play Marlowe's theme of tragic love is

[1] Brian Morris, ed. *Christopher Marlowe, Mermaid Critical Commentaries,* 1968.

re-enacted . . . and above all the quality of dramatic effect of Dido's sublime erotic rhetoric informs the inner life and movement of Cleopatra's poetic imagination.'[1] This is, perhaps, rather to overstate the case. But if Hamlet had this play in mind in his discussion with the players, it is clear what a lasting effect it had on Shakespeare's imagination. Indeed, it is not too much to say that his imagination was saturated with Marlowe. At the same time Dr. Gibbons remarks: 'The excessive degree of hyperbole is disturbing, carries suggestions of hysteria and distorted eroticism'—often of sadism, in fact, which comes out most clearly in Aeneas's relation of the sack of Troy and in a few other rather nasty touches. Sadism is most obviously present in *Tamburlaine* and finds overt expression in the Hitlerian vaunts of the Scourge of God himself. Like Hitler, Tamburlaine makes good the cruellest and most outrageous of his boasts—literally using Bazajeth as his footstool and harnessing the conquered kings to his chariot. It is a quality which makes this play such a sickening spectacle on the stage.[2] We are no longer amused when Tamburlaine has Bajazeth brought on in his cage to entertain him while he eats his dinner, nor when he advises him either to feed off his own arms or to eat his wife before she gets too thin from starvation. But it evidently amused an Elizabethan audience. This is one aspect of Marlowe's sense of humour. A more recent production of *The Jew of Malta* by the Royal Shakespeare Company also showed it for what it was—a black comedy full of

[1] "Unstable Proteus": *The Tragedy of Dido Queen of Cathage, Mermaid Critical Commentaries,* 1968.
[2] As last performed at the Old Vic by Donald Wolfit in 1951.

equally sick humour motivated by an utter contempt for the human race. In performance *Edward the Second* is just as theatrically effective, and the very speed with which events follow one another until their final culmination in overwhelming horror appeals to modern directors, for the play as a whole fits nicely into the modern conception of the Theatre of Cruelty, just as *The Jew* can be seen as an early example of the Theatre of the Absurd. Both these factors explain the modern cult of Marlowe and sharply distinguish him from even the early Shakespeare—but we should not forget his horrific *Titus Andronicus*.

Though many critics have come to regard *Edward the Second* as Marlowe's most mature play, I am myself in agreement with J.B. Steane, who finds it Marlowe's most depressing play. 'The depressing quality seems to me to be virtually omnipresent and to lie in two pervasive characteristics', writes Mr. Steane. 'One is the unredeemed meanness, weakness and wickedness of the people and their actions; the other is the drab thinness of the verse'.[1] It is more depressing than *The Jew* because its characters are nearer to human beings, whereas the latter is not unlike a glorified Punch and Judy show. The very hopelessness of *Edward the Second* may be an indication that Marlowe had reached the end of his tether. It may even be his last play. Whether it was followed by *Doctor Faustus* or not we cannot be sure, though the exalted lyricism of *Faustus* would suggest a date nearer to *Tamburlaine*. In which case we should have to assume an earlier date than 1592

[1] *Christopher Marlowe: The Complete Plays*, Penguin edition, 1969.

for P.F's translation of the *Faustbook,* which is described on the title page as 'newly imprinted'.

But what do the plays tell us of Marlowe's attitude to the society of his own time? This seems to have been, as Professor Knights observes, one of 'exasperation and contempt', as appears unequivocally in *The Jew of Malta,* with its reflections on Elizabethan 'policy' and its greed of power and money. 'Marlowe's sardonic intelligence is genuinely engaged with what actually goes on in his world—a world where either you eat or are eaten, and where unction is a sure sign of corrupt purpose.'[1] One has only to look at the hawk-like and rapacious faces of Elizabethan nobles, as shown in their portraits, to see how correct Marlowe was in his diagnosis. Yet he was himself, to a large extent, at the mercy of the unresolved conflicts in his own nature, which he was unable to control by his analytic, rational intelligence. It is this which makes him appear so contradictory and largely accounts for the ambivalent tone of his work. That Marlowe should sometimes baffle his critics is only to be expected, for he baffled and outraged his contemporaries. They saw him as an atheist, an Epicurean, and a Machiavellian. As a Renaissance man, Marlowe was fascinated by the concept of power, only to become aware of its illusory nature:

But what are kings when regiment is gone
But perfect shadows in a sunshine day?

as his Edward II ruefully reflects.

His tragedies bear eloquent witness to the disintegration of the Humanist ideal of the dignity and

[1] L.C. Knights, 'The Strange Case of Christopher Marlowe', *Further Explorations.*

excellence of man, a theme developed in the next century by Chapman and Webster, Marlowe's heirs.[1]

Such is the picture of Marlowe that emerges from contemporary studies, and it is also one that is implicit in the present book. For all his theatrical skill in distancing his subject matter, I see no reason to modify my earlier view of him as a subjective writer, an 'insatiable speculator' like his own Faustus, who used the drama for the expression of the same views as he maintained in his familiar conversation. Since this book was written, however, Marlowe's plays have been more frequently performed. From these later presentations it is evident that they are no less relevant to our own age than Shakespeare's, perhaps in some respects even more so. As Mr. James Smith has observed: 'The Marlowe of the theatre is terrifyingly modern. Can the Marlowe of the more academic critics boast as much?'[2]

Following what he calls 'proper historical method', Dr. Rowse claims to have 'added a new chapter to Marlowe's life' by identifying him with the Rival Poet of Shakespeare's *Sonnets* and confidently states that Marlowe's Leander is a recognisable portrait of the Earl of Southampton.[3] For both these assertions there is precious little evidence, though this particular Rival Poet theory has been put forward from time to time by others, notably by Oscar Wilde in *The Portrait of Mr. W.H.* But, very little of material value about Marlowe has come to light since Dr. Urry's discoveries in the Canterbury city records, while the rival theories that have been advanced to account for

[1] M.M. Mahood, 'Marlowe's Heroes', *Poetry and Humanism,* 1950.
[2] 'The Jew of Malta' in the Theatre, *Mermaid Critical Commentaries.*
[3] A.L. Rowse, *Christopher Marlowe: A Biography, 1964.*

his death rest on no more than supposition. Deductions about his character from the evidence of the plays and poems has proved to be a more fruitful field of inquiry, from Dr. Paul Kocher and Professor Harry Levin onwards. The outlines of a strongly individual mind and temperament do emerge, combining to form the type of mind known in his own times as the Overreacher—'That like I best that flies beyond my reach . . . Although my downfall be the deepest hell'. In these lines, spoken by the Duke of Guise in *The Massacre at Paris*, we have the essence of the man.

BOOKS PUBLISHED SINCE 1952

The place of publication is London, unless otherwise stated.

ARMSTRONG, W.A., *Marlowe's 'Tamburlaine': The Image and the Stage*, Hull, 1966.

BROCKBANK, J.P., *Marlowe: Dr. Faustus*, 1963.

CLEMEN, W., *English Tragedy before Shakespeare*, English trans. 1961.

COLE, D., *Suffering and Evil in the Plays of Christopher Marlowe*, Princeton, 1962.

CRAIK, T.W., ed. *The Jew of Malta*, 1966.

JUMP, J.D., ed. *Tamburlaine the Great*, 1962; *Marlowe's 'Dr. Faustus'*: A casebook, 1969.

FORD, B., ed. *A Guide to English Literature Vol. II, The Age of Shakespeare*, 'The Plays of Christopher Marlowe' by J.C. Maxwell, 1955.

HENDERSON, P., *Christopher Marlowe*, Writers & Their Work, 1972.

KNIGHTS, L.C., 'The Strange Case of Christopher Marlowe', *Further Explorations*, 1965.

LEECH, C., 'Marlowe's Edward II: Power and Suffering', *Critical Quarterly 1*, iii, 1959; ed. *Marlowe: a Collection of Critical Essays, Twentieth Century Views*, Prentice Hall, New Jersey, 1964.

LEVIN, H., *The Overreacher: A Study of Christopher Marlowe*, 1954.

MACLURE, M., ed. *Christopher Marlowe: The Poems*, 1968.

MORRIS, B., ed. *Christopher Marlowe*, Mermaid Critical Commentaries, 1968.

OLIVER, H.J., ed. *The Tragedy of Dido Queen of Carthage*, 1968.

ORGEL, S., ed. *Christopher Marlowe: The Complete Poems and Translations*, 1971.

ROWSE, A.L., *Christopher Marlowe: A Biography*, 1964.

SANDERS, W., *The Dramatist and the Received Idea, Studies in the Plays of Christopher Marlowe*, 1968.

STEANE, J.B., *Marlowe: A Critical Study*, Cambridge, 1964; ed. *The Complete Plays*, Penguin Books, 1969.

THURSTON, G., Inquest—Christopher Marlowe's Death, *Contemporary Review* March/April 1964.

URRY, W., 'Marlowe and Canterbury', *Times Literary Supplement*, February 13, 1964.

WILSON, P.F. *Marlowe and the Early Shakespeare*, Oxford, 1953.

WRAIGHT, A.D., and Stern, V., *In Search of Christopher Marlowe: A Pictorial Biography*, 1965.

ERRATA

p.50 line 24: for 'Berowne' read 'the king'.
p.52. The quotations from *Love's Labour's Lost*
should read: lines 8–9: 'Small profit have continual
plodders ever won'; lines 12–15:
These earthly godfathers of heaven's lights
   That give a name to every fixed star,
Have no more profit on their shining nights
   Than those that walk and wot not what
   they are.
p.139 line 28: delete the second 'Hero'.

Chapter One

CANTERBURY

CHRISTOPHER MARLOWE is the one English poet
in whom was most fully incarnated the spirit of
the Italian Renaissance. He had much of the Florentine
elegance and subtlety of mind; his lines are clear and
radiant with the eager intellectual climate of his time.
'His raptures were,' said Drayton, 'all air and fire.'
In his nature was combined in almost equal degree the
ardour of the poet and the critical analytic faculty.
These two elements, in their conflict, made up the
meteoric being that was Marlowe.

The Canterbury city records of the Marlowe family
have been traced back to 1414, when William Morle,
a fuller, became a freeman of the city on the payment
of ten shillings.[1] A Christopher Marle, or Marley, of
Westgate Street, a tanner, died in 1540, leaving his
wife pregnant. In his will he bequeathed to the unborn
child, 'if it be a man child, my dwelling house and the
hangings of the house, the meat table, the best chair,
and a house joining to my dwelling house called the
Old Hall with the land longeth thereto in fee simple.'
To his widow, Joan, he left the tannery and twenty
acres of land at Hackington. It is usually assumed that

[1] The name Marlowe occurs in various forms in contemporary documents:
Marlo, Marley, Marlin, Morley, Merling. John Marlowe, the poet's father,
habitually signed himself 'Marley.' Christopher does the same in his one
surviving signature.

the man child, born in the year of his father's death, was John, the father of Christopher Marlowe the poet. John was born at Ospringe, a village near Faversham, where the parish records have unfortunately been destroyed. In the various depositions which give his place of birth, John Marlowe is rather vague as to the date. He is just as vague about the date at which he originally came to Canterbury and also about how long he had lived in St. George's parish. If he really was the son of the Christopher Marley who died in 1540, he was evidently heir to some considerable property, though by 1564 he was no longer living in his father's house in Westgate Street.

About 1560 John Marlowe was apprenticed to Gerard Richardson, shoe-maker. The trade of shoe-making was associated in the same Canterbury guild with the family trade of tanning. While still an apprentice, John married, at the church of St. George the Martyr, Catherine Arthur, possibly the daughter of the Revd. Christopher Arthur, sometime rector of St. Peter's, ejected under Queen Mary as a married minister. John Marlowe became a freeman of the city in 1564, on payment of 4s. 1d., though the usual period of apprenticeship was seven years. In the first fourteen years of their married life Catherine gave birth to nine children, four boys and five girls. Two of the boys died in infancy and there is no further record of the second Thomas who was baptized in 1576. But Margaret, Joan, Ann and Dorothy survived and married local tradesmen. Two of the children, it will be noticed, bore the names of their probable grandparents.

Christopher Marlowe, the eldest son and the second child of this marriage, was baptized on 26 February 1564 at St. George's church. Local tradition used to point to a house standing at the corner of St. George's Street and St. George's Lane as his birthplace, but as a matter of fact it has never been proved that John Marlowe lived in this particular house, which was destroyed by fire in June 1942 during one of the German air raids on the city. Since eight of his children were baptized at St. George's, John Marlowe must have lived in the locality. In 1564, as appears from the Hunt-Applegate libel case, he had two apprentices working in his shop.[1]

It is often said that Marlowe was the son of 'a poor cobbler.' But there is sufficient evidence of at least a moderate middle-class prosperity in his home, comparable to the early environment of William Shakespeare, who was baptized on 26 April 1564 at the market town of Stratford. By comparison, Canterbury was a whirlpool of dangerous life. Until the Reformation it had been a centre of pilgrimage to the tomb of St. Thomas Becket, 'the holy blisful martir,' from whose shrine Henry VIII's commissioners carried away twenty-six cartloads of gold and jewels. But in spite of the depredations of reforming zeal—or rather, the greed of the new commercial monarchy—Canterbury was still, when Marlowe was born there, to all outward appearances the same little mediaeval town of churches and priories, dominated by the great cathedral and encircled by the walls, with their six double-towered gates and twenty odd watching towers. The halfway resting place on the road from Dover to London, its hostelries were equipped to receive the suites of ambassadors and through its streets streamed the Queen's ragged, unpaid and embittered soldiery, returning from her continental wars. There were three public gibbets in Canterbury. The third was put up, evidently to meet a pressing need,

[1] See page 5.

in 1576. Otherwise, while these were still tenanted, men were hanged on the city walls from the condemned cell in an upper room of Westgate. This seems to have impressed Marlowe as a boy, for in *Tamburlaine* the Governor of Babylon is hung up in chains on the city walls and shot to death. 'See, my lord,' exclaims Tamburlaine's son, 'how brave the captain hangs!'

Certainly life in Canterbury was 'brave' in those days. In the middle of the town stood the bull's stake, to which bulls were tied in order to be baited and torn to bits by dogs. The Burghmote even passed a decree that no meat might be sold in the open market unless the animal had first been baited by bull dogs. Public executions of the most revolting kind were still fresh in the memory of the citizens. Under 1540 the city account books itemize the sums paid out to the various people engaged in the hanging and parboiling of Friar Stone, who had refused to acknowledge Henry VIII as supreme head of the church. 'Item paid to ii men that fet [fetched] the ketill & parboyled him xiid; Item paid to iii men that caryed his quarters to the gates & sett them up xiid; Item paid to a woman that scowred the ketyll iid; Item paid to him that did execucyon iiiis. viiid.'[1] It may be that Marlowe was drawing upon this event in the annals of Canterbury when he made Barabas fall into a boiling cauldron in the last scene of *The Jew of Malta*. He did not have to go very far afield for the more atrocious incidents in his plays, and, conversely, the Elizabethan appetite for horrors was fully catered for by the dramatists. Shakespeare's divine pity for human weakness and suffering is not characteristic of Elizabethan drama as a whole, though it is this quality which brings him nearer to us than any

[1] John Bakeless, *The Tragicall History of Christopher Marlowe*, I. p. 38.

of his contemporaries. For Marlowe, scenes of cruelty seem to have been a source of exhilaration. His friend Thomas Nashe was also very representative of the age in this combination of lyrical sensibility and sadism, for it would be hard to parallel the gusto with which he describes the death by torture of Cutwolfe in *The Unfortunate Traveller*.

But there is another side to the picture—the youthful high spirits and abounding happiness of the townsfolk in Dekker's *The Shoemaker's Holiday*. John Marlowe may not have been another Simon Eyre, nor Catherine Marlowe quite so simple as Dame Margery, but the life depicted by Dekker, though doubtless idealized, cannot have been so very different from the atmosphere of Marlowe's home. In a contemporary law case, we read that during a walk to Barham in the year 1563 Lawrence Applegate, a tailor, had confessed to John Marlowe, 'I have had my pleasure of Goodwife Chapman's daughter.' Not content with this indiscreet avowal, Applegate continued to boast of his conquest 'at divers times and in sundry places,' adding that Goodwife Chapman owed him two shillings and that as she now refused to pay him back he had 'occupied' her daughter four times, 'which was for every time 6d.' Applegate seems to have been pleased with the twist he had given to the affair, for he repeated his story in the presence of Mistress Marlowe and their two apprentices, and again at the house of the father of one of the apprentices.[1]

As a freeman of the city of Canterbury, John Marlowe had the right 'to come to the council of the same city, and there speak and be heard, where others shall be void and put away.' He also had the right to be tried

[1] Bakeless, op. cit. I. pp. 24–5.

'for any trespass' by a Canterbury jury and not to be
condemned or convicted by 'foryn men,' or imprisoned
anywhere but in Canterbury. Freemen had a monopoly
of the city's trade. But there were responsibilities as
well as privileges. Freemen were required to contribute
to the defence of the city and to provide 'one armed
pike to be kept for use if needful.' In the year of the
Armada, when his son's Tamburlaine was scourging
kingdoms with his conquering sword and harnessing
kings to his coach on the London stage, John Marlowe
appears in the city records as a member of the second
platoon of Canterbury archers who left to join the
trained bands to fight the Spaniards.[1] He signed his
will with his mark and this was taken as evidence of his
illiteracy until the discovery of his signature as John
Marley on several legal documents.

When Christopher was ten years old, the family
moved from the eastern parish of St. George's to the
parish of St. Andrew in the centre of the town, in the
neighbourhood of the bull's stake (which stood just
outside the precincts of the cathedral) and Pillory
Lane. Here John Marlowe became a professional
bondsman on behalf of couples seeking marriage licences.
On 28 April 1579 he became security for no less a sum
than £100. About 1588 he moved again, to the parish of
St. Mary's, where he became churchwarden. There is no
doubt about the respectability of the Marlowes. On his
death, John Marlowe left all his 'temporal goods' to
his wife. The entry of his burial on 26 January 1605
in the register of St. George's (he directed that he
should be buried where he was married forty-three
years before) describes him as 'clerk of St. Maries.'

[1] Discovered by W. G. Urry, Keeper of the Manuscripts, Canterbury
Cathedral Library.

Of Marlowe's mother we know little, beyond the fact that, if she was the daughter of a clergyman, she may have been of a slightly higher social rank than her husband. Her will, executed on 17 March 1606, shows her to be living in comfortable circumstances and to be a careful and methodical housewife. This will gives us the only direct glimpse we can hope to get of the Marlowe household. Mistress Marlowe bequeathed to her married daughters, Margaret Jurden, or Jorden, Ann Crawford and Dorothy Cradwell, and to her friends or household servants, gold and silver rings ('the greatest gold ring' and 'the ring with the double posy'), a collection of silver spoons, silk cushions, christening linen, tablecloths ('and the fourth to go for an odd sheet that he which hath the sheet may have the tablecloth'), six pairs of sheets, a dozen napkins ('to be divided equally because some are better than other'), pillow-coats, gowns and petticoats ('my red petticoat' and 'my petticoat that I do wear daily and a smock and waistcoat'). Special pride is taken in the silver spoons and they are separately specified. Her daughter Joan, who married at the age of thirteen, may have been dead by this time, for she is not mentioned in the will; but Joan's husband, John Moore, is left forty shillings and 'the join press that standeth in the great chamber where I lie.'

On 14 January 1579, a few weeks before he was fifteen, Christopher Marlowe entered the King's School. He was only just in time, for it was laid down in the statutes that no boy should be admitted who had exceeded his fifteenth year. In the second quarter of 1579 the name 'Christopher Marley' appears in the accounts of the Treasurer of the cathedral as the recipient of the quarterly allowance, due to King's scholars, of £1. From earliest times the King's School had been attached to the cathedral, in whose precincts it still stands. When Henry VIII drove out the monks of Canterbury in 1541, the school was given a royal title to mark the occasion and a new governing body set up. Since then the King's School has been repeatedly enlarged. The buildings form a quadrangle round the Mint Yard with an entrance gate of 1545 and there is now a Marlowe House. Most of the old buildings were destroyed in the middle of the nineteenth century to make room for the School House, the laboratories and the gym, but the famous Norman staircase still stands, as do some mediaeval domestic buildings.

In Marlowe's time the pupils were to be 'fifty poor boys, both destitute of the help of friends, and endowed with minds apt for learning, who shall be sustained out of the funds of the Church.' Boys were not admitted until they could read and write and they were maintained for four or, at most, five years 'until they have obtained a moderate acquaintance with the Latin grammar, and have learned to speak in Latin and write in Latin.' As a matter of fact, the boys were no more confined to the sons of what used to be called 'the poor' than are the Bluecoat boys of today. When Cranmer visited the school in 1541, the majority of the boys were the sons of the local gentry and he objected that: 'If the gentleman's son be apt to learning, let him be admitted; if not apt, let the poor man's child [that is] apt enter [in his] room.' Lessons began at six in the morning with a psalm and concluded in the same manner at five in the afternoon. Each boy was provided with a midday meal and 2½ yards of cloth for a new gown at Christmas. At Christmas, too, the boys acted plays, probably in Latin, as this was a favourite way of teaching

fluency in the language. When Elizabeth visited Canterbury in August 1573, she was greeted at the cathedral
door with an oration by 'a grammarian'—perhaps one
of the King's schoolboys. She put up at the priory of
St. Augustine and stayed a fortnight, bumping through
the cobbled streets of the city in her coach with its
ostrich plumes, a stiff and glittering image surrounded
by the gentlemen pensioners with their gilt battle-axes.

At the age of sixteen, Marlowe was ready for the
university, and at the close of the Michaelmas term of
1580 he went up to Corpus Christi, Cambridge, on
one of the scholarships founded by Matthew Parker,
Archbishop of Canterbury and Master of Corpus, for
'the best and aptest scholars well instructed in their
grammar and if it may be such as can make a verse.'

Chapter Two

CAMBRIDGE

CORPUS CHRISTI is one of the oldest colleges in Cambridge. Here, among the grey walls and green lawns, Marlowe had six and a half years of study. When he went up in December 1580 what is now called the Old Court comprised the entire college, the Trumpington street frontage not being added till the Gothic Revival. Corpus then stood, as it still stands, between two churches—the ancient St. Benet's and St. Botolph's. The ecclesiastical atmosphere was, therefore, even more pronounced at Cambridge than at Canterbury.

Archbishop Parker had bequeathed to Corpus his magnificent library of Saxon and Early English manuscripts, assembled to demonstrate the ancient and continuous traditions of the English Church. Though a staunch Protestant, Parker disliked the Puritans, 'those irritable precisians of Cambridge.' Calvinism had spread rapidly at the university in the 1560's and 70's, and the authorities complained of the 'nicknaming and scoffing at religion' and the debauched and atheistical opinions of the students, who, they said, fooled about in chapel, made up nonsensical prayers and turned in the wrong direction during the Creed.

Besides Calvinism, all forms of free and rational thought were in the air at Cambridge, and the literatures of Rome, France and Italy were eagerly studied. Gabriel Harvey, in a letter to Spenser of 1579, the year before

Marlowe went up to the university, writes: 'You cannot step into a scholar's study but (ten to one) you shall likely find open either Bodin de Republica or Leroy's Exposition upon Aristotle's Politics or some other like French or Italian political discourses. And I warrant you some good fellows amongst us begin now to be prettily well acquainted with a certain parlous book called, as I remember me, Il Principe di Nicolo Machiavelli, and I can peradventure name you an odd crew or two that are as cunning in his Discorsi, in his Historia Fiorentina, and in his Dialogues della arte della Guerra too, and in certain gallant Turkish discourses. . . .' In another letter from Cambridge to Spenser of April 1580, Harvey reverts to the same theme: 'The French and Italian when so highly regarded by scholars? The Latin and Greek, when so lightly? . . . Turkish affairs familiarly known.'[1]

Turkish affairs provided Marlowe with material for *Tamburlaine* and *The Jew of Malta*, and he was clearly influenced by both Bruno and Machiavelli. Whether he read these authors himself (and there is no reason why he should not have done so, with this widespread Elizabethan enthusiasm for everything Italian), or whether he was influenced by them indirectly, it is not so easy to decide. It would seem, from the fragmentary nature of his work, that Marlowe was too rash and impatient by nature for careful scholarship, or even for prolonged application to any subject, though intellectually brilliant. Given his peculiar temperament, he would naturally pick up all the boldest and most advanced ideas of his time, the more revolutionary the better. He would be delighted to find Bruno calling Christ a carpenter and treating Greek and Christian legends,

[1] Grosart, *The Works of Gabriel Harvey*, I. pp. 137–8; 69–70.

in the *Spaccio*, on the same level; or to read in Ramus's
De Religione that Moses was an Egyptian braggart and
the Christians dunces and scoundrels.[1] But there are
direct traces of Bruno's and Machiavelli's influence
in his plays. The heroic frenzy of *Tamburlaine* would
seem to derive straight from Bruno's *De gli eroici furori*[2]
and, as Eleanor Grace Clark has pointed out, both the
prose and verse of Bruno is shot through with the
'conceit' frequently used by Marlowe—that which
represents a mortal spirit longing to be resolved into
the spirit of the elements.[3] Again, in the dedication
of *Eroici Furori*, Bruno exalts the love of philosophy above
the love of women. When Marlowe brings Machiavelli
on to the stage in the Prologue to *The Jew of Malta*, he
makes him say things that may be found in popular
distortions of his writings by Gabriel Harvey and Gentillet. On the other hand, his lifelong concern with what
men did as compared with what they believed, or
professed to believe, derives from Machiavelli's empiri-
cism, as does the peculiarly ironic humour which
emerges from the contrast of these two positions.
The clear, realistic temper of much of Marlowe's
writing, and his destructive rationalism, are close to
the Florentine's. *The Jew of Malta* could hardly have
been written without a knowledge of Machiavelli.
Nor, for that matter, could *The Massacre at Paris*.

Unfortunately, it is of the more humdrum side of
Marlowe's academic career that we know most. Patient
research has revealed to Mr Bakeless that 'Marlen'
spent a penny at the buttery on his arrival at Cambridge

---

[1] Poirier draws attention to the fact, in his *Christopher Marlowe*, that Gabriel
Harvey noted down these remarks of Ramus (Pierre de la Ramée) in his
Marginalia. Marlowe, at any rate, never forgot them.

[2] Benvenuto Cellini, *Marlowe*, p. 19.   [3] *Ralegh and Marlowe*, p. 35.

in the second week of December 1580. Next week
he was rash: he spent 3s. ¾d.—three times the amount
allowed to him for his weekly buttery bills. He did
not formally matriculate till 16 March 1581, when an
entry in the University Matriculation Register reads:
'Coll. Corp. Xy. Chrof. Marlen.' But he appears
to have been regarded as a scholar before either his
matriculation or his formal election. In a list dated
29 October 1581, 'Merling' appears as one of the
Corpus Christi undergraduates in the class of 'Mr
Johnes, Professor lecturae dialecticae.' At this period
the subject of dialectics was exciting special interest
and controversy at Cambridge, where the University
was divided between the adherents of the traditional
Aristotelian system and the followers of the 'French
Plato' Petrus Ramus, who attacked Aristotle and
based himself on Plato as expounded by the Florentine
humanists. Echoes of these academic debates are found
in both *Doctor Faustus*, where Faustus's definition of the
aim of logic, *Bene disserere est finis logicae*, is taken from
the *Dialectica* of Ramus,[1] and in *The Massacre at Paris*,
where the Duke of Guise defends Aristotle before con-
temptuously ordering Ramus to be stabbed. In any case,
William Temple's edition of Ramus of 1584, dedicated
to Sidney, must have been known to all students at
Cambridge.

Under the terms of Archbishop Parker's will, the
King's School scholars nominated by him were to
occupy 'that room or chamber in the said college late
called a Storeroom now repaired and finished for that
purpose at the cost and charge of the said John Parker'—
that is, Archbishop Parker's son. The Storeroom was
situated on the ground floor at the north-west angle

---

[1] F. S. Boas, *Christopher Marlowe*, p. 16.

of what is now the Old Court. The Master and Fellows of the college agreed to give Parker's nominees 'reading in the hall within the said college, their barber and launder freely without anything paying therefore' and 'to use the said scholars in such convenient order and manner as other scholars.' They were not to be absent for more than a month a year, except on college business or through sickness. For every week of absence a scholar forfeited his allowance of a shilling. As the college Buttery Books and the record of the scholarship payments show, Marlowe not only spent more than his shilling allowance in some weeks, but came and went more or less as he pleased.

In theory, undergraduates were very closely confined. They were not supposed to go outside the college gates unless accompanied by a member of the college; and inside they were required to talk to one another in Latin or Hebrew, and they were not allowed to read irreligious books or to keep 'fierce birds.' All taverns, fairs, dances and public sports, and 'all such things that allure and entice them to lewdness, folly and riotous manners, whereunto the nature of man is more inclined,' as the Privy Council wrote to the college authorities, were out of bounds. These rules were enforced by severe penalties, such as flogging and the stocks. 'Poor scholars,' such as Marlowe, were required to be 'honest, lowly, studious and such as might become their station,'[1] and all students were supposed to wear a priestly gown reaching down to their heels made of 'woolen cloth, or black puke, London brown, or other sad colour.'

---

[1] Technically, Marlowe was a pensioner, or ordinary student. Above him were the fellow commoners, the sons of the nobility, who behaved exactly as they liked; below him, the sizars were the really poor students, who performed menial tasks in return for board and education.

In practice, the richer students, according to William Harrison, in his *Description of England*, used to 'ruffle and roist it out, exceeding in apparel and riotous company, which draweth them from their books unto another trade. And for excuse, when they are charged with breach of all good order, think it sufficient to say they are gentlemen, which grieveth many not a little.' These gentlemen, adds Father Parsons, wore excessive ruffs, clothes of velvet and silk, swords and rapiers, contrary to academic rules; playing at cards and dice in the parlours of inns and engaged in fencing, cock-fighting and bear-baiting. To this disgraceful laxity he attributes 'the filling up and pestering of colleges with harlots to be baits for the young men.'

We have the evidence of Robert Greene, Marlowe's senior by two years, who had returned to St. John's in 1583 to take up his M.A. degree after a tour of Italy and Spain, that at Cambridge 'I light among wags as lewd as myself, with whom I consumed the flower of my youth.' In Italy, he said, he had practised 'such villainy as is abhominable to declare.' Thomas Nashe matriculated to St. John's in October 1582 as a sizar at the age of fifteen. He says, in the preface to Greene's *Menaphon* (1589), that his college was famous throughout the university for its passionate addiction to learning, 'having (as I have heard grave men of credit report) more candles light in it, every winter morning before four of the clock, than the four of clock bell gave strokes.' Since no fires were provided in undergraduates' rooms, this was proof of a veritable humanistic rage.

Until his second year 'Marlin' was in permanent residence at Cambridge. But he was apparently absent for six weeks during the fourth term of this year and for seven weeks during the third term of 1583. In his fourth year he was again uninterruptedly in residence, but in his fifth year, 1585, he appears to have been absent a good deal. During at least one of these absences, in April 1585, he was at Canterbury, for there he witnessed the will of Catherine Benchkyn, in the company of Thomas Arthur, possibly an uncle, John Moore, his brother-in-law, and his father, thus providing us with his one surviving signature.[1] The scholarship accounts for 1586 are missing, but the entries in the Buttery Book for that year show that, except in the third term, Marlowe was in regular attendance.

He took his B.A. during his fourth year and became 'Dominus Marlin.' In the University Grace Book for 1584 'Christof. Marlyn' appears second in a list of twelve Corpus Christi men admitted to the degree; in order of seniority he is 199th among 231 under-graduates—not a very brilliant record. The fact that after taking his B.A. the scholarship payments go on for another three years is evidence that Marlowe intended —or, at least, gave out that he intended—to take Holy Orders, for the Parker scholarships were only renewable on that condition. Later he made Faustus think:

> Having commenced, be a divine in show,
> Yet level at the end of every art.

And probably this was the course adopted by Marlowe himself. The translation of Ovid's *Amores*, usually considered to be the work of his undergraduate years, is not an occupation one would normally associate with a divinity student. It is a line for line rendering in heroic couplets, one of the most lively ever done.

---

[1] Discovered in 1939 by F. W. Tyler, former sub-librarian, Canterbury Cathedral Library.

L. C. Martin, in his edition of Marlowe's *Poems*, has shown that many of the apparent mistranslations are exact renderings of the sixteenth-century editions which Marlowe used. *Ovids Elegies*, as they are called on the undated edition purporting to be issued at Middleburgh in Holland, were bound up with Sir John Davies's bawdy epigrams. The unnamed printer evidently wanted to save himself from prosecution and at the same time to sell the book on its scandalous appeal. It was publicly burned at Stationers' Hall on 4 June 1599 by order of the Archbishop of Canterbury and the Bishop of London —'a brace of prelates,' Swinburne calls them—soon after the burning of the books in which Nashe and Gabriel Harvey had so uproariously abused one another.

To the Cambridge years also, perhaps, belongs the translation of the first book of Lucan. Just as the sunny erotic world of *Hero and Leander* is prefigured in *Ovids Elegies*, so certain lines of the Lucan suggest *Tamburlaine*. There is a tradition that Marlowe also translated Coluthus's *Rape of Helen* in 1587. No copy of this translation survives, but in the previous year Thomas Watson, one of Marlowe's friends, had published a Latin version, *Helenae Raptus*. Certainly the play *Dido, Queen of Carthage* would seem to be a direct result of these classical studies. Much of it is a line for line translation of the *Aeneid*, though it is here that Marlowe's authentic accent sounds for the first time in Dido's cry

> For in his looks I see eternity,
> And he'll make me immortal with a kiss.[1]

In March 1587 'grace' was granted to 'Ch. Marley' to proceed to his M.A. But such alarming reports of his activities now began to reach the university authorities

---

[1] cf. *Antony and Cleopatra*, I. iii. 'Eternity was in our lips and eyes . . .'

that, at the last moment, they refused him permission to take up his degree. Indeed, it was rumoured that he intended to join the English Catholics at Dr. Allen's seminary for the training of Jesuits at Rheims. At this point Marlowe must have appealed to some influential patron, for a Privy Council resolution of 29 June 1587 was thereupon dispatched to Cambridge. 'Whereas,' wrote their lordships, 'it was reported that Christopher Morley was determined to have gone beyond the seas to Rheims and there to remain their Lordships thought good to certify that he had no such intent, but that in all his actions he had behaved himself orderly and discreetly whereby he had done Her Majesty good service, and deserved to be rewarded for his faithful dealing. Their Lordships request that the rumour thereof should be allayed by all possible means, and that he should be furthered in the degree he was to take this next commencement: Because it was not Her Majesty's pleasure that anyone employed as he had been in matters touching the benefit of his country should be defamed by those that are ignorant of the affairs he went about.'

Marlowe returned to Cambridge, took his M.A. in July, and by the end of the year both parts of *Tamburlaine the Great* had been presented on the stages of London.

Chapter Three

GOVERNMENT SERVICE

MARLOWE, the Privy Council stated, had 'in all his actions . . . behaved himself orderly and discreetly . . . and deserved to be rewarded for his faithful dealing.' His employment was evidently of a secret and confidential nature, and it had given rise to rumours that he 'was determined to have gone beyond the seas to Rheims and there to remain.'

A seminary for English Catholic youth had been founded by Dr. (later Cardinal) William Allen at Douai some years earlier, but in March 1587 it was moved to Rheims, owing to the hostile attitude of the Protestant Flemish. As we know from the Cambridge play *The Pilgrimage to Parnassus*, poor scholars, seeing no future for themselves in England, went over to Rheims or Rome and sought employment under the banner of the Counter-Reformation. Such employment sometimes involved returning to England as missionary priests, inciting English Catholics to civil war and, perhaps, even participating in plots to kill the Queen. Francis Walsingham, therefore, sent his spies over to Rheims, Rome and Paris to watch and report.

Pius V's excommunication of Elizabeth in 1570 had placed English Catholics in a terrible dilemma: they had to choose between renouncing their faith and celebrating Mass in their own homes in a perilous secrecy. But it was only after the discovery of Jesuit plots that the calculated mildness of the Elizabethan settlement gave way to an increasingly bitter persecution of Catholics, and the reason for this was political, not religious. Fear of Rome was well grounded. The Massacre of St. Bartholemew and the murder of Henry III in France had thoroughly frightened the authorities, and they were determined to prevent such a state of affairs arising in England.

One way of preventing it took the form of an elaborate espionage system, a giant spider's web covering the whole country, at the centre of which sat Mr. Secretary Walsingham, with Phelippes as his decipherer and forger and Topcliffe as his officer. Richard Topcliffe, however, did not really come into his own until after Walsingham's death in 1590, when, as the Queen's man, he was allowed to keep a private rack in his house in Westminster churchyard for the examination of recusants, both men and women, because 'the often exercise of the rack in the Tower was so odious, and so much spoken of by the people.' He boasted that he had a machine of his own invention which made the common rack child's play in comparison. Topcliffe's fiendish cruelty to Fr. Robert Southwell excited such indignation, even among Protestants, and so numerous were the complaints to the Privy Council, that Cecil had him arrested and temporarily imprisoned on the pretence that he had, in this particular case, exceeded his authority. He was soon at large again, however, touring the country in search of 'massing priests'— bribing servants, corrupting children and searching country houses. Threatened with his warrant, no one was safe, no house free from his sudden visits. Topcliffe and his agents, we read, regarded that day as lost in which they did not 'bag' a Jesuit or a massing priest in this sport of 'topcliffizare,' as it was familiarly known at Court. When prisons overflowed, country houses were requisitioned for the reception of recusants, and many Catholics came to know that dark cellar infested with rats below river level at the Tower. Queen Elizabeth herself was not above accepting the hospitality of her Catholics subjects and then having them arrested at the end of her visit.[1]

Among Walsingham's young men was a certain Richard Baines, whose activities would seem to have been very typical of many others. This Baines may very well be the same Richard Baines who informed against Marlowe in the summer of 1593. Between 1578 and 1582 he had been living a stealthy life as a spy at Dr. Allen's seminary at Rheims. A year before, he was ordained priest and began celebrating Mass and hearing confession. In 1583 he decided to return to England and disclose what information he had gathered, through confession and otherwise, to Walsingham, and to this end he asked Allen for leave and journey money to return to his native country as a Catholic propagandist. He told a confederate that Walsingham would give each of them 3,000 crowns for their information. Another of Baines's plans was to kill off the entire seminary by poisoning the well, like Barabas in *The Jew of Malta*. Unfortunately for him his confederate proved less 'resolute' and disclosed the whole design to his superiors. As a result, Baines spent ten months in the town gaol and during his imprisonment made a full confession of his treachery.[2]

[1] e.g. Edward Rookwood of Euston Hall, near Thetford, arrested during Elizabeth's progress through Norfolk in 1578. Topcliffe was present on this occasion.

[2] F. S. Boas, 'Informer against Marlowe,' *Times Literary Supplement*, 16 September 1949.

Anthony Munday, the dramatist and pamphleteer,
also went to Rheims on the same business as Baines and
there collected information against Fr. Campion. He
also attended executions at Tyburn and wrote them up
in pamphlet form, exulting particularly in the sufferings
of the saintly Campion, whom he had helped to bring
to the scaffold. He also went to Rome and on his
return wrote an account of the English Catholics at
the seminary there, *The English Romain Life*. Later he
appears in Henslowe's diary as a busy dramatist, writing
for the Admiral's company between 1594 and 1602.
Another informer, Robert Poley, was one of the men
with whom Marlowe spent the last day of his life at
Deptford. In 1583 Poley was living in Walsingham's
house at Barn Elms as Sir Philip Sydney's man—put there
by the Catholics to spy upon 'Mr. Secretary'—Sidney
having recently married Walsingham's daughter, Frances.
In 1586 Poley, working in conjunction with Ballard, a
seminary priest from Rheims, was mainly responsible for
incriminating Anthony Babington in a plot against the
Queen's life.[1] It was at Poley's lodgings, immediately
after a visit by Thomas Walsingham, that Ballard was
arrested.

Poley's activities, as spy and *agent-provocateur*, seem
to have been particularly complicated and double-faced.
He was indeed the 'perfect Machiavel.' Like Baines, he
managed to pass himself off as a sincere Catholic, was
in the confidence of Mary, Queen of Scots, and secured
the affections of the naïve and charming young Babington deeply enough to bring him to the gallows. Next
year Poley was still working with Thomas Walsingham,

[1] It was he who worked Babington up to the pitch of writing his letter of
7 July 1586, to Mary Queen of Scots, which disclosed the whole extent of
the plot.

for he refers to another meeting with him in Seething Lane, 'where I attended Mr. Thomas Walsingham for my secret recourse to Mr. Secretary.' From 1588 onwards the Accounts of the Treasurer of the Chamber contain a series of payments to him as an accredited messenger to and from English ambassadors, state agents and courts abroad, and the ciphers which he used in his correspondence have been identified. In 1591 there is a reference to him as living in Shore-ditch. He may have been the Robert Pollye of Clare College, Cambridge, who was a chorister of King's in 1564. If so he was a good deal older than Marlowe. He had secretly married 'one Watson's daughter' but in 1589 he was involved in a suit for the alienation of the affections of Joan Yeomans, the wife of a London cutler, whom he entertained at 'fine banquets' in the Marshalsea prison.[1]

Another spy, Gifford, had taught theology at Rheims. Working with Poley, he encouraged Babington to pursue his plot and, it has been suggested, inserted those passages in Mary Stuart's letters to Babington while acting as her messenger that finally brought her to the scaffold. Before her execution, he fled to Paris where, in 1588, he was arrested in a brothel and imprisoned by the Bishop of Paris. After bringing serious charges against the English ambassador, who had tried to procure his release, he died in prison in 1590. Gifford came of a Catholic family himself and his father had been imprisoned as a recusant.

But Catholics, though the worst, were not the only sufferers. Munday, between 1588 and 1590, acted as

---

[1] The Watson who was Poley's father-in-law may have been Marlowe's friend, Thomas Watson, the poet. It is characteristic of Poley's double-dealing that he should have been married by a seminary priest.

Whitgift's chief Martinist hunter. The virulent pamphlets of the Martinists attacked the Anglican bishops as 'petty popes, and petty usurping anti-christs,' pointing ironically at Whitgift's sumptuous palace and the troupe of gold-chained attendants who served him on their bended knees as a modern example of Christian humility. Whitgift himself superintended the examination and torture of suspected Martinists and it was Munday's job to nose round the booksellers in St. Paul's Churchyard and Blackfriars, listen to the conversation of people who might be Puritans and rummage in the packs of the country carriers in the hope of discovering the whereabouts of the Martinists' printing press.

It was from this corrupt and feverish world that Marlowe chose some of his friends. Elizabethan writers were, it should be remembered, driven to desperate shifts in order to keep alive at all. Robert Greene went in for coney-catching, others became spies. Marlowe's government service was, perhaps, no more than that of a messenger employed to carry dispatches to and from English ambassadors and state agents abroad. One 'Morley' is, in fact, mentioned in a letter of 2 October 1587 from Utrecht to Lord Burghley as such a messenger. Again, we find 'Marlin' referred to as a messenger between the government and Sir Henry Unton, British Ambassador in Paris in 1592.[1] Messengers were expected not only to carry dispatches, but to report on the condition of the countries they passed through, with any other information which might be useful to the government. And during the Armada years it was the activities of English Catholics abroad that particularly interested Her Majesty's government.

[1] Poirier, *Christopher Marlowe*, p. 25.

If Marlowe's government service brought him into contact with Catholics, as it most likely did, for it may have been of much the same nature as Poley's, what more natural than that he should be suspected to be one? The dramatist in him was evidently attracted by the Catholic ritual, for Baines reports him as saying, 'That if there be any God or good religion, then it is in the papists, because the service of God is performed with more ceremonies, as elevation of the Mass, organs, singing men, shaven crowns etc.' Marlowe must have seen these ceremonies on the Continent. That his government service took him abroad seems to be borne out, too, by casual references in his plays. *The Massacre at Paris*, particularly, shows an intimate acquaintance with French politics.

During these years the French embassy in Butcher Row (a narrow street running into the Strand near the site of the present Law Courts) was seething with spies and intrigue. It was through the French embassy that Mary, Queen of Scots, communicated with her friends abroad, Walsingham having obligingly supplied her with beer barrels in which to conceal her letters. But the letters went to Walsingham before delivery at Butcher Row. Frances Yates thinks that John Florio, the translator of Montaigne and secretary to Mauvissière, was probably working all the time for Walsingham.[1] Giordano Bruno was also living at the French embassy during his patron Mauvissière's residence there, when anti-French demonstrators plastered its windows with filth, used even more filthy language to the Ambassador's household, and stopped up the drains so that the house became uninhabitable.[2] Bruno replied in

[1] *John Florio*, pp. 84–5. When Chateauneuf replaced Mauvissière as ambassador in 1585, he requested Florio to live somewhere else.

[2] Ibid. pp. 63–4.

kind when he wrote that the English populace was 'a sink,' 'an excrementitious mob.' As Poley worked as Mary Stuart's courier, he was doubtless well acquainted with the French embassy and its inmates.

From Elizabethan times until quite recently, the profession of spy, or secret agent, has been regarded as something rather unpleasant and vaguely unworthy of 'a man of letters.' In our own age, with its war of ideologies and its more frankly Machiavellian view of politics, and its atmosphere of purges, concentration camps and the secret police, spies have come back into favour again. We are thus in a better position to-day to understand Marlowe and the atmosphere in which he worked than our immediate ancestors, who lived in a state of security which they took for granted. The morality of a nation fighting for its life, as England was in the age of Elizabeth, is very different from the attitude of a country whose predominance in world affairs in unquestioned.

To one of Marlowe's turn of mind there would be much to attract him in secret service work, for he seems to have continued in it for the rest of his life, which partly accounts for his small literary production. It had the romantic glamour of the sinister, the excitement of the perilous; it also gave him first-hand experience of the kind of 'policy' which inspired *The Jew of Malta*. Poley and Thomas Walsingham remained his friends until that fatal day at Deptford, and Poley is one of the more sinister figures in the underworld of Elizabethan politics. Marlowe's attitude to this work may be summed up by Barabas, when he says:

> Haply some hapless man hath conscience
> And for his conscience lives in beggary.

Young Spencer's words to Baldock in *Edward II* have much the same ring of conviction:

> Then Baldock, you must cast the scholar off,
> And learn to court it like a gentleman.
> Tis not a black coat and a little band,
> A velvet cap'd cloak, fac'd before with serge,
> And smelling to a nosegay all the day,
> Or holding of a napkin in your hand,
> Or saying a long grace at a table's end,
> Or making low legs to a nobleman,
> Or looking downward, with your eyelids close,
> Or saying, 'Truly an 't may please your honour!'
> Can get you any favour with great men.
> You must be proud, bold, pleasant, resolute,
> And now and then, stab as occasion serves.

The stabbing seems to be almost a part of the pleasantry, and Kyd was later to accuse Marlowe of 'rashness in attempting sudden privy injuries to men,' just as Gabriel Harvey was to write of his peacock pride and the ostentation of his dress. Such a man would surely find in Ralegh his ideal hero. To the injunctions of Young Spencer, Baldock replies, as Marlowe himself might have done while still an undergraduate at Cambridge, that though he had to be 'curate-like' in his attire, he was 'inwardly licentious enough' and 'apt for any kind of villainy.'

Chapter Four

NEWGATE

CHRISTOPHER MARLOWE and William Bradley were fighting with drawn swords in Hog Lane, Finsbury, on the afternoon of 18 September 1589, between two and three o'clock. When Thomas Watson intervened to part the combatants, Bradley cried out: 'Art thou now come? Then I will have a bout with thee!' and turned upon him with sword and dagger. Watson defended himself with his sword as best he could against the furious attack, giving ground and backing towards a ditch. Cornered and already wounded, he grew desperate and of a sudden ran his adversary through the breast, inflicting a wound six inches deep of which Bradley immediately died. Attracted by the shouts and the cries of other people in the street, Stephen Wyld, the constable, arrived on the scene. He arrested Marlowe and Watson and took them before Sir Owen Hopton, the Lieutenant of the Tower, then living in Norton Folgate. Hopton committed both prisoners to Newgate to await trial at the next sessions of Old Bailey.[1]

The man whom Marlowe fought and Watson killed was the son of the host of the Bishop Inn, which stood at the junction of High Holborn and Gray's Inn Lane. At the age of nineteen, Bradley had been badly wounded

[1] Mark Eccles, *Christopher Marlowe in London*, from which most of the information in this chapter is drawn.

in the shoulder in a fight with an apprentice. Five years later, in 1586, he was in another skirmish and his neighbours in Gray's Inn Lane, a carter and a tailor, bound themselves as securities for him at £5 each, and he himself gave bond to the extent of £40 that he would in future keep the peace. The quarrel which ended in his death had its origin in a debt. In 1588 Bradley had bound himself under a penalty of forty marks to pay John Alleyn, inn-holder and brother of Edward Alleyn the actor, the sum of £14. Next year the debt was still unpaid, and Bradley had to secure himself against assault from Alleyn, Hugo Swift and Thomas Watson. But, as we have seen, this precaution proved useless.

There were three Hog Lanes on the outskirts of the City in Elizabethan times. The longest ran from Aldgate High Street to Bishopsgate and had become a favourite site for surburban development. The Hog Lane in which Marlowe and Bradley fought is, however, described in the coroner's inquest as in the parish of St. Giles without Cripplegate. It can therefore only have been the Hog Lane which began at Norton Folgate and ran west through Finsbury Fields to the north of the present Finsbury Square.

Among the entries in the register of prisoners who arrived at Newgate between 9 September and 2 October 1589 we find:

> Thomas Watson nuper de Norton ffowlgate in comitatu Middlesex generosus & Christoferus Marlowe nuper de eadem yoman. . . .

Both Marlowe and Watson, then, lived in Norton Folgate, a suburban district with, says Stowe in his *Survey of London*, 'many fair houses builded, for receipt and lodging of worshipful persons.' Outside Bishopsgate, Norton Folgate ran northwards, as it still does, into Shoreditch, the theatrical district. It was in Holywell Street (now Holywell Lane and Holywell Row), a turning off Shoreditch to the west, that three years later Marlowe got into trouble again: this time for assaulting the constables.

The inquest on Bradley was held at Finsbury on the day after the duel and a jury of twelve decided that Watson had killed him in self-defence. Then both prisoners were returned to Newgate to await their trial. As a poet Thomas Watson was ranked by his contemporaries with Sidney and Spenser. He was also the most famous Latin poet of his day and a prolific playwright. Meres describes him in *Palladis Tamia* as one of the best for tragedy, though other references stress his wit. The author of *Ulysses upon Ajax* speaks of Harington's etymologies as 'the froth of witty Tom Watson's jests, I heard them in Paris fourteen years ago: besides what balductum play is not full of them.' From 1576–7 Watson was studying law at Douai, and his association with Walsingham in Paris in 1581 (a period affectionately recalled in his *Meliboeus* of 1590) suggests that Mr. Secretary's spy ring included yet one more man of letters. It was most likely Watson who introduced Marlowe to Walsingham in the first place; and if he is the Watson whose daughter Robert Poley married— a ceremony performed secretly in Bow Lane—Poley had evidently decoyed the girl as he decoyed many other people. By 1587 Watson was living in St. Helen's Bishopsgate, as we know from the curious and pathetic case of Ann Burnell, in which he gave evidence and is there referred to as 'a wise man of St. Helen's.' (Ann Burnell was finally whipped barebacked through the

City at a cart-tail, for giving out that she was the king of Spain's daughter, by reason of some curious marks on her backside that at the full moon had the appearance of the Royal Arms of England.) Altogether, Watson had spent seven or eight years at the universities of France and Italy. His *Amintas* is based on Tasso; he produced the first collection of Italian madrigals in English; and he speaks with admiration of Bruno in the Dedication to the *Compendium memoriae localis*, fearing that compared with the 'mystical and deeply learned *Sigillis* of the Nolan or with the *Umbra artificiosa* of Dicson' his little work 'may bring more infamy to its author than utility to the reader.'[1] He was, therefore, a man imbued with Italian culture and his influence on the young Marlowe must have been considerable. After the Hog Lane affair both men shared the same cell at Newgate.

On his arrival at this loathsome place, a felon was first manacled, then put in a dungeon known as Limbo, the condemned hold over the prison gate. This 'dark opace wild room,' entered by a hatch from above, was completely dark except for a candle set on a stone, against which a desperate man had once dashed out his brains. Newgate had a grim reputation. Luke Hutton, a prisoner there in the same year as Marlowe and Watson, has left a description of the place in *The Black Dog of Newgate*, of its darkness, its rat-infested cells, its starving men in irons begging most piteously for bread—a spectacle that amused the gaolers, who suggested that 'he lay too soft who lay on ground.' A scholar, it is related in the notes to the 1638 edition of Hutton's pamphlet, committed for 'charms and devilish witch-crafts' in the reign of Henry III was 'by the famished

[1] Singer, *Giordano Bruno*, p. 40.

prisoners eaten up' and had since then haunted the prison in the shape of a black dog. What with foul water, bad sanitation, bad food, over-crowding and the general filthiness, more prisoners died from gaol fever than were executed by the law. But for a garnish, or fee, the gaoler would strike off a prisoner's leg-irons, secured to his waist by an iron hoop, and give him a choice of lodging in the master's or the common side, according to how much he could afford to pay for the privilege. On the master-felon's side the chief occupation was drinking in a vaulted cellar known as 'the Boozing ken.' When he had spent all his money in trying to forget his misery, a prisoner went back to the common side, or to the underground Stone Hold.

As a wounded man, the plight of Thomas Watson in such a place is hardly imaginable. Marlowe, as later reported by Richard Baines, occupied himself by learning to make counterfeit coins. 'He was acquainted with one Poole, a prisoner in Newgate, who hath great skill in the mixture of metals, and having learned such things of him, he meant, through the help of a cunning stamp-maker, to coin French crowns, pistolets and English shillings.'

On 1 October Marlowe was admitted to bail. 'Richard Kytchine of Clifford's Inne, gentleman, & Humfrey Rowland of East Smithfeilde in the county aforesaid, horner, came before me, William Fleetwoode, Serjeant at Law and Recorder of the City of London, one of the Justices of our Lady the Queen appointed in the county aforesaid, & became sureties for Christopher Marley of London, gentleman: to wit, each of the sureties aforesaid under the penalty of twenty pounds, and he, the said Christopher Marley, undertook for himself, under penalty of forty pounds . . . on condition that he the said Christopher shall personally appear at the next Sessions of Newgate to answer everything that may be alledged against him on the part of the Queen, and shall not depart without the permission of the Court.' Fortunately, Marlowe never seemed to be in want of either friends or money in an emergency. Richard Kitchen was an attorney who later did a certain amount of legal work for Philip Henslowe, the proprietor of The Rose theatre. He was also a friend of William Williamson, the host of the Mermaid Tavern in Bread Street. (It was at the Mermaid that Ralegh founded a literary and philosophical club and it may have been here that he taught the young man who would not stop talking such a salutary lesson. This young man, says Aubrey, 'made a noise like a drum in a room. So one time in a tavern, Sir W. R. beats him and seals up his mouth, i.e. his upper and nether beard, with hard wax.') Humphrey Rowland, Marlowe's other surety, was a manufacturer of shoe-horns, lant-horns and knife-handles. For several years Rowland had been one of the constables of the district. In 1586 he was churchwarden of St. Botolph's and next year he recorded in the parish register, 'we did ring at our parish church and for joy that the Queen of Scots that enemy of our most noble queen and majesty was beheaded for the which the Lord God be praised.' Kitchen, rather than Rowland, is more likely to have been Marlowe's friend.

On 3 December Marlowe and Watson were summoned to the Old Bailey. On the bench sat Sir Roger Manwood, Chief Baron of the Exchequer, who had an estate near Canterbury and upon whom at his death Marlowe wrote a Latin epitaph; Sir John Harte, the Lord Mayor; William Fleetwood, who in 1594 bought one of the

D

early editions of *Tamburlaine*;[1] Chief Justice Wray of the Queen's Bench; and Anderson of the Common Pleas. Anderson, we are told, had the reputation of looking upon prisoners with a strange fierceness and discouraging them still further by violent invective. 'I pray you, let us make short work of him,' he remarked to his fellow judges at the trial of the Puritan writer John Udall.

The justices having nothing against Marlowe, he was discharged with a warning to keep the peace, and they found no reason to doubt that Watson had killed Bradley in self-defence. Watson was, however, returned to Newgate until 12 February 1590 to await the Queen's pardon. He survived his release two and a half years, living in Bishopsgate as tutor to the son of William Cornwallis and writing plays. After his death, Marlowe commended his memory to the Countess of Pembroke in a prose dedication, signed 'C.M.,' to *Amintae Gaudia*. Nashe also paid homage to him in *Have With You to Saffron Walden*: 'A man he was that I dearly loved and honoured, and for all things hath left few his equals in England.'

A wry reference to Marlowe in Robert Greene's *Menaphon*, published in 1589, may have had its origin in these events. Greene writes of him as the teller of 'a Canterbury tale; some prophetical full-mouth that as he were a cobbler's eldest son, would by the last tell where another shoe wrings.'

---

[1] Bakeless, op. cit. pp. 160–1.

Chapter Five

THE SCHOOL OF NIGHT

THE plague was still about and the theatrical companies were on tour in the autumn of 1592, and
Robert Greene lay dying of a surfeit of pickled herring
and Rhenish wine taken in company with his friend
Thomas Nashe. To pay for this 'fatal banquet' he had
had, it is said, to pawn his sword. Soon afterwards
he was picked up penniless in the streets by a cobbler's
wife, who took him home and gave him a bed in her
garret at Dowgate. 'The king of the paper stage, the
monarch of cross-biters, and the very emperor of
shifters.' So Gabriel Harvey describes him after his death
in the masterly invective of *Four Letters*. 'Who in London
hath not heard of his dissolute and licentious living;
his fond disguising of a Master of Arts with ruffianly
hair, unseemly apparel, and more unseemly company:
his vainglorious and thrasonical braving: his piperly
extemporizing, and Tarletonizing: his apish counter-
feiting of every ridiculous and absurd toy: his fine
cozening of jugglers, and finer juggling with cozeners:
his villainous cogging and foisting: his monstrous
swearing, and horrible foreswearing: his impious
profaning of sacred texts: his other scandalous and
blasphemous ravings: . . . his infamous resorting to
Bankside, Shoreditch, Southwark, and other filthy
haunts: his obscure lurking in basest corners. . . . They
that have seen much more than I have heard, can relate

35

strange and almost incredible comedies of his monstrous disposition, wherewith I am not to infect the air, or defile this paper.'

But now, syphilitic, dropsical, verminous and deserted by his friends, as Greene lay in extreme pain and poverty in the shoe-maker's garret, he began to reflect upon his past life, and the prospect appalled him. He died, with his autobiographical novel, *Greene's Groatsworth of Wit, Bought with a million of Repentance*, unfinished. Its publication was the greatest 'sensation' in literary circles of September 1592, for it contained an address 'To those Gentlemen his Quondam acquaintance that spend their wits in making plays'. No one was actually named, but Marlowe, Peele and Nashe were distinguishable. 'Wonder not (for with thee will I first begin) thou famous gracer of tragedians,' he wrote to Marlowe, 'that Greene, who hath said with thee (like the fool in his heart) There is no God, should now give glory unto His Greatness; for His Hand lies heavily upon me; He hath spoken unto me with a voice of thunder, and I have felt He is a God that can punish enemies. Why should thy excellent wit, His gift, be so blinded, that thou shouldst give no glory to the Giver? Is it pestilent Machiavellian policy that thou hast studied? O peevish folly! What are his rules but mere confused mockeries, able to extirpate in small time the generation of mankind. For if *Sic volo, sic jubeo* hold in those that are able to command: and if it be lawful *Fas et nefas* to do anything that is beneficial [i.e. to oneself], only Tyrants should possess the earth, and they striving to exceed in tyranny, should each to the other be a slaughter man; till the mightiest outliving all, one stroke were left for death that in one age man's life should end.' [A correct diagnosis of the power politics practised by Marlowe's supermen and a remarkable forecast of the atomic age.] 'The broacher of this diabolical atheism [Machiavelli] is dead, and in his life had never the felicity he aimed at; but he began in craft, lived in fear, and ended in despair. . . . This apostate perished as ill as Julian: and wilt thou, my friend, be his disciple? Look but to me, by him persuaded to that liberty, and thou shalt find it in an infernal bondage. I know the least of my demerits merit this miserable death, but wilful striving against known truth, exceedeth all the terrors of my soul. Defer not (with me) till this last point of extremity: for little knowest thou how in the end thou shalt be visited.' A prophetic utterance, as it happened, for Marlowe was to follow Greene to the grave within a year of this warning, and in a manner that looked to many of his contemporaries very like an act of God.

It is impossible, even now, to read this strange document without being moved. Its value for Marlowe's biography consists in the fact that Greene is throughout addressing him as a friend in the sincerity of his heart, as one who was familiar with his beliefs and way of life. As early as 1588, in the preface to *Perimedes*, he had written of Marlowe as 'daring God out of his heaven with that atheist Tamburlain' and as the author of 'impious instances of intolerable poetry.' But *The Groatsworth* was no longer motivated by envy of Marlowe's success. Greene was now speaking the truth, as he saw it, more in sorrow than in anger. 'Base-minded men all three of you,' he concludes, 'if by my misery you be not warned.'

Next, he warned his friends against the players— 'those puppets, I mean, that speak from our mouths, those Antics garnished in our colours. Is it not strange that I, to whom they all have been beholding, is it not like that you, to whom they all have been beholding, shall (were ye in that case as I am now) be both at once of them forsaken? Yet trust them not: for there is an upstart Crow, beautified with our feathers, that with his *Tiger's heart wrapt in a Player's hide*, supposes he is as well able to bombast out a blank verse as the best of you: and being an absolute *Johannes fac totum*, is in his own conceit the only Shake-scene in a country. O that I might entreat your rare wits to be employed in more profitable courses: & let those Apes imitate your past excellence, and never more acquaint them with your admired inventions.'

From Chettle's *Kind Heart's Dream*, published in December, we learn that Greene's warnings and imputations were 'offensively taken' by both the famous gracer of tragedians and the upstart crow. Chettle's opinion of Marlowe could, by implication, scarcely be more bluntly expressed: 'With neither of them that take offence was I acquainted, and with one of them I care not if I never be.' To Shakespeare, however, he apologises: 'I am as sorry as if the original fault had been my fault, because myself have seen his demeanour no less civil than he excellent in the quality he professes. Besides, divers of worship have reported his uprightness of dealing, which argues his honesty, and his facetious grace in writing, that approves his art.' But as for Marlowe, 'whose learning I reverence, and at the perusing of Greene's book, struck out what then, in conscience, I thought he in some displeasure writ: or had it been true, yet to publish it was intolerable, him I would wish to use me no worse than I deserve.' We might have learned a good deal more about Marlowe from Greene if Chettle had not exercised his editorial discretion, though his use of the word 'intolerable' may indicate that Greene had anticipated in the *Groatsworth* the charges of atheism and blasphemy made later by Baines and Kyd. At any rate, the publication of the *Groatsworth* created a scandal and when Nashe was charged with having written it he replied that it was 'a scald, trivial, lying pamphlet.'

But Marlowe had other friends and connections than these. There are clues which connect him with Ralegh. But though he was reported to be on intimate terms with several of Ralegh's immediate circle, Harriot, Warner and Roydon, and though Ralegh wrote a reply to his *Passionate Shepherd*, the only direct evidence we have of any actual association between the two men comes from an informer's report of May 1593 on the activities and opinions of Richard Chomley, one of Marlowe's secret service friends who had been employed by the Privy Council 'for the apprehension of Papists and other dangerous men.' From *Remembrances of words and matter against Richard Cholmeley*, a document among the Harleian MSS. in the British Museum, we learn that Chomley 'said and verily believeth that one Marlowe is able to show more sound reasons for atheism than any divine in England is able to give to prove divinity, and that Marlowe told him that he hath read the atheist lecture to Sir Walter Ralegh and others.' It rather looks as though Marlowe had written an actual treatise on what was then known as atheism, and this finds some support in an entry in Henry Oxinden's commonplace book to the effect that 'Mr Fineux of Dover was an atheist . . . he learned all Marloe by heart and divers over books.' Again, Thomas Beard in *The Theatre of God's Judgement* (1597) says that Marlowe 'denied God and his son Christ, and not only in word blasphemed against the Trinity, but also (as it is credibly reported) wrote a book against it, affirming Our Saviour to be a deceiver, and Moses to be a conjuror and seducer of the people, and the Holy Bible to be but vain and idle stories, and all religion but a device of policy.'

If Marlowe really had Ralegh as a friend, he could not have found anyone more inspiring. With his legendary reputation, his fantastic magnificence, his subtle and daring mind, he was one who seemed to live and have his being in the world of the creative imagination itself. He was almost Tamburlaine in the flesh, 'he had that awfulness and ascendency in his aspect over other mortals,' writes John Aubrey. There was something slightly incredible about Ralegh and to his contemporaries he seemed a man of more than normal stature. The patron of Spenser, Drayton, Jonson and Harriot, he discussed archaeology with Camden and alchemy with Dr. Dee; he is reported to have sat up all one night with a Jesuit in prison arguing about his faith; Hakluyt was much indebted to him for his *Principal Navigations*; yet the bulk of his 'most lofty, insolent and passionate' poetry is lost, his *History of the World* is unfinished and his dreams of empire came to nothing. His aspirations were too high and he seems to have possessed all qualities in excess.

Ralegh was the Queen's favourite for about six years, from 1582 until the arrival of Essex in 1587. In 1592, however, he lost her favour by marrying Elizabeth Throckmorton, one of the Maids of Honour. He was recalled from the Panama expedition and dispatched, with his wife, to the Tower, where he fell into a frenzy at being denied the Queen's presence. Earlier in the year, he had written to Cecil: 'I protest before God, there is none, on the face of the earth, that I would be fastened to.' He was released after about two months, in September 1592, to supervise the unloading at Dartmouth of the Portuguese carrack, the *Madre de Dios* whose capture off the Azores was largely the work of his own ships. The prize amounted to some £150,000, of which the Queen took the greater part, Ralegh only being allowed a small share which barely covered his expenses. Nevertheless, the money softened the Queen's heart and she set him at liberty. In a letter to the Treasury, Ralegh remarked caustically: 'Four score thousand pounds is more than ever a man presented to her Majesty as yet.' But he was still forbidden to come to Court, and retired to Sherborne Abbey, one of the Queen's earlier gifts to him, where he occupied himself in rebuilding and laying out the grounds.

Soon dangerous rumours began to circulate about the free thought and heretical opinions current at Sherborne. Nashe is evidently referring to these in his *Piers Penniless* (1592), when he remarks on 'a number of them that fetch the articles of their belief out of Aristotle, and think of heaven and hell as the heathen philosophers,[1] take occasion to deride our ecclesiastical state, and all ceremonies of divine worship, as bugbears, scarecrows, because (like Herod's soldiers) we divide Christ's garments among us into many pieces, and of the vesture of salvation make some of us babies' and apes' coats, others strait trusses and devil's breeches. . . . Hence atheists triumph and rejoice, and talk as profanely of the Bible as of *Bevis of Hampton*. I hear say there be mathematicians abroad, that will prove men before Adam, and they are harboured in high places who

[1] cf. 'My ghost be with the old philosophers'—*Doctor Faustus*.

will maintain it to the death that there are no devils.'[1]

These rumours were given further substance by the pamphlet *Responsio ad Elizabethae Edictum* of the same year, which commented on the severe edict against Catholics of 1591, by 'Andreas Philopater,' who has been identified with Father Parsons. 'And certainly,' wrote Parsons, 'if the popular school of Atheism of Walter Ralegh shall have made but little further progress (which he is said to maintain in his own house notoriously and publically, with a certain necromantic astronomer as tutor, so that no small crowds of noble youth have learned to mock both the Old Law of Moses and the New Law of Christ Our Lord with certain witty jests and quips, and to laugh at them in their Society), if this school, I say, should take root and strength, and Ralegh himself should be chosen to the Senate, whereby he may direct also the business of the Commonwealth (which all expect, and not without the highest probability, since he holds the first place in the Queen's eyes after Dudley and Hatton, and all see that from almost all the crowd of soldiers from Ireland he had been made chief man and powerful without any previous merits by favour of the Queen alone): what else, I say, must be expected than that we may even see at the same time some edict ordained by that magician and epicurean tutor of Ralegh, and proclaimed in the Queen's name, whereby all divinity, all immortality of the soul and expectation of another life may be lucidly, clearly, briefly, and beyond a per-

[1] Harriot's Mathematical Papers contain calculations on the chronology of the Book of Genesis and the age of Adam. Much of what Nashe writes, however, reads as though he were repeating Marlowe's table-talk as reported by Baines: 'he persaudeth men to atheism, willing them not to be afeard of bugbears and hobgoblins.'

adventure, denied, and those accused of high treason as if they were troublers of the Commonwealth who have any occasion for scruple against a doctrine of that nature, so easy-going and kindly to those who now wallow in the vices of the flesh.' Parsons also referred to Ralegh as 'a courtier too high in the regard of the English Cleopatra,' who wore in his shoes jewels worth 6600 gold pieces.

A summary of the *Responsio*, printed abroad, was then issued in English, *An Advertisement written to a Secretary of my lord Treasurer's of England*, in which we read once more of 'Sir Walter Ralegh's School of Atheism by the way, and the conjuror that is master thereof, and of the diligence used to get young gentlemen to this school, wherein both Moses and Our Saviour, the Old and the New Testaments are jested at, and the scholars taught among other things, to spell God backward.' It is evident, of course, to any reader of his poems, his *History of the World*, or his essays *The Sceptic* and *The Soul*, that Ralegh was far from being what is now known as an atheist, but in those days the term was given to any kind of free or rational thinker. In an age of religious fanaticism, Ralegh stood almost alone for religious toleration and intellectual liberty. When, in 1592, the Puritan John Udall, who had dared to criticize the bishops of the Anglican Church, was sentenced to death for high treason, Ralegh got him reprieved, though in fact he died soon after in the Tower as the result of torture. As M.P. for St. Michael in Cornwall, Ralegh made a stand in the House of Commons in April of the same year against a Bill proposing to put all Brownists (that is, extreme Puritans) to death. 'The law', he said, 'is hard that taketh life, or sendeth into banishment, when men's intentions shall be judged by a

jury, and they shall be judges of what a man meant.'
Ralegh was also above racial prejudice. He said that
the ladies of Guiana and of Elizabeth's Court were
indistinguishable in their manners, and he sternly in-
sisted that his men should treat them with courtesy
and, furthermore, should pay in kind for everything they
took. Two hundred years later the 'Indians' still looked
for his return. He had become a legend in Guiana.

At Durham House, Strand, Ralegh received in his
book-lined turret overlooking the Thames men of
learning and intellect of all classes. He was on terms
of familiarity with Mauvissière, Marquis de Castelnau, the
French Ambassador, and the generous and enlightened
patron of Giordano Bruno during the latter's residence
in England from 1583–5. In a letter to his secretary,
John Florio, of September 1585 Mauvissière instructs
him to call upon 'Monsieur de Raglay' and present an
invitation to supper at his house on the following day.
These suppers at the French Embassy were attended
by such men as Sidney, Fulke Greville and the members
of what came to be called 'The School of Night.' Here
scientific and philosophical discussions took place
similar to that recorded in Bruno's *Cena de le ceneri*
(*Ash-Wednesday Supper*). Though the scene of this is
laid at Fulke Greville's house in Whitehall, Bruno told
the Venice Inquisition in 1592, that the gathering in
question was under Mauvissière's roof.[1]

In the *Cena de le ceneri*, Bruno reaches the supper
party only after stumbling knee-deep through the mud
in one of the pitch-black lanes leading up from the
Thames to the Strand (their surly boatmen having
refused to take them any further) and after being insulted
and set upon as a foreigner at Charing Cross by the usual

[1] Frances Yates, *John Florio*, p. 97.

'excrementitious mob of rowdies.' A recently discovered first draft of the opening dialogue proves that Bruno was taken to the supper by Florio and Matthew Gwynne, with whom Florio shared a love of music as well as letters. 'And they told him that this knight was most desirous of conversing with him, being particularly eager to learn the reasons for the movement of the earth and other paradoxes firmly held by him [Bruno], and also very anxious to understand the conceits of Copernicus.'[1] At supper the atmosphere grows heated when Bruno gives his reasons for believing that the earth moves and that there are innumerable universes and peopled worlds similar to our own. The party breaks up altogether after he has confuted an Oxford doctor, who draws an inaccurate plan of the Copernican universe.

It is quite possible that these scientific supper parties at the French Embassy, during Bruno's and Mauvissière's residence there, were the origin of Ralegh's 'School of Night.' Harriot's familiarity with Bruno's works has been proved from a note among his *Mathematical Papers* and the letters to him from his disciple Sir William Lower. Harriot not only grasped the Copernican theory, but advanced it; his most important contribution to science being his study of the nature of light and the allied problem of optics. It is hardly by chance that Marlowe was so preoccupied with the aspect of the heavens, the movement of the planets, and the intoxicating qualities of light. His interest in witchcraft and demonology, too, probably derived from the 'School of Night.' His sense of infinity and the latent metaphysical tone of his work came more directly from Bruno, whom he resembled in revolu-

[1] Frances Yates, *John Florio*, p. 93.

tionary ardour. Astronomy was for Marlowe always the most exalted of sciences.

Bruno wrote of himself: 'The Nolan has given freedom to the human spirit, and made its knowledge free. It was suffocating in the close air of a narrow prison-house, whence, but only through chinks, it gazed at the far off stars.' This was to be his own lot, once he fell into the hands of the Church, for they kept him shut up for eight years, before burning him. Bruno believed that both matter and spirit were indestructible and of a divine substance, a unity informed by immanent Mind—a conception echoed in *Tamburlaine*. Ralegh's circle also shared Bruno's admiration for Pythagoras—whose theory of metempsychosis is despairingly invoked by Faustus as an alternative to that eternity of torment promised by the Christian church. Most significant of all is Bruno's conception of 'heroical spirits,' for whom true learning and philosophy constitute the highest happiness; such spirits, despising both the love of women and the vulgar paths trodden by the schoolmen, follow their own inward illumination of superior knowledge. All these qualities are, as a matter of fact, attributed by Peele, in *The Honour of the Garter*, to the 'wizzard' Earl of Northumberland, who was also a well-known patron of Harriot and much taken up with experimental science, alchemy and occultism.

With his pride, his intolerance of mediocrity and conformism and his 'atheism,' Ralegh had become at this time almost the most unpopular man in England. Ballads were made up about him:

> Ralegh doth time bestride,
> He sits 'twixt wind and tide,
> Yet uphill he cannot ride,
> For all his bloody pride.

The man referred to by Parsons as a magician and a conjurer and master of Ralegh's 'school of atheism' was, of course, none other than Thomas Harriot, the most distinguished English mathematician before Newton. We find Harriot writing to Kepler, deploring having to live in an age when it was impossible either to think or write freely, and he is reported to have been had up before the Privy Council for denying the resurrection of the body. Harriot's other conjuring tricks included observations made through his 'perspective trunks.' His discoveries and the scientific and rational tone he gave to the Ralegh coterie inevitably cast some doubt upon the literal interpretation of the Bible, and this is echoed in the opinions attributed to Marlowe by Baines and others. Aubrey writes that Harriot 'did not like (or valued not) the old story of the Creation of the World. He could not believe the old position: he would say *ex nihilo nihil fit* (from nothing nothing is made). He made a philosophical theology wherein he cast off the Old Testament, and then the New one would consequently have no foundation. He was a Deist. His doctrine he taught to Sir Walter Ralegh and Henry Earl of Northumberland and some others.' Besides Harriot, Aubrey names Walter Warner and Robert Hues (two of the best mathematicians in England) as members of Ralegh's circle, and Kyd told Puckering that Harriot and Warner were those with whom Marlowe conversed.[1]

Reports and rumours from Sherborne so alarmed the authorities that they sent spies into Ralegh's household to keep them informed of his private conversation, and in March 1594 they set up a Commission at Cerne Abbas headed by Lord Thomas Howard to make

[1] See p. 59.

a full enquiry. But though the depositions revealed an attitude to religion that could scarcely be called either orthodox or pious, the evidence proved to be of too vague and general a character to warrant prosecution and the matter was dropped. One of the clergymen who gave evidence said that 'about some three years past coming to Blandford out of Hampshire his horse was stayed and taken for a post horse by Sir Walter Rawleigh and Mr Carew Rawleigh.' When he objected that he needed it to get home as soon as possible to preach, the next day being Sunday, Carew Ralegh replied that he 'might go home when he would, but his horse should preach before him.' Francis Scarlett, minister of Sherborne, said that as he was passing a local shoemaker's shop 'about Christmas last,' the shoemaker called him in and complained that although Scarlett preached that there was a God, a heaven, a hell and a resurrection, 'there is a company about this town that say, that hell is no other but poverty and penury in this world; and heaven is no other but to be rich, and enjoy pleasures; and we die like beasts, and when we are gone there is no more remembrance of us.' Worse still, Thomas Allen, Lieutenant of Portland Castle, had once torn two leaves out of the Bible to dry tobacco on and had been heard to curse God for sending rain to spoil his hawking—saying 'a pox on that God which sendeth such weather to mar our sport.' Allen was reported to be 'a great blasphemer and light esteemer of religion' and 'when he was like to die, being persuaded to make himself ready to God for his soul,' he answered 'that he would carry his soul up to the top of an hill, and run god, run devil, fetch it that will have it.'

The most interesting piece of evidence, however,

was the deposition of the Rev. Ralph Ironside, who said that he was dining at Sir George Trenchard's house at Wolverton in the summer of 1593 in company with Sir Ralph Horsey, Ralegh and Carew Ralegh, when Horsey had occasion to rebuke Carew Ralegh for 'some loose speeches.' Ironside had said that one could not be too careful how one spoke about sacred subjects, lest one found oneself damned body and soul, and Carew Ralegh had replied: 'Soul, what is that?' Ironside told him that it was better to think about how the soul might be saved than to be too curious in enquiring of its essence. Whereupon Sir Walter asked him if he would not, 'for their instruction,' answer the question put to him by his brother. 'I have been, saith he, a scholar some time in Oxford, I have answered under a Bachelor of Art, and had talk with divines, yet hitherunto in this point (to wit what the reasonable soul of man is) have I not by any been resolved. They tell us it is *primus motor*, the first mover in a man &c.' Ironside sought to satisfy Ralegh with Aristotle's definition of Anima, but Ralegh objected that the Aristotelian definition was 'obscure and intricate.' Ironside answered that the soul was a spiritual and immortal substance breathed into man by God. 'Yea, but what is that spiritual and immortal substance? said Sir Walter. The soul, quoth I. Nay then, saith he, you answer not like a scholar.' Ironside said that arguments about first principles must necessarily proceed in circles; whereupon Ralegh objected that on the contrary mathematical principles could be proved by demonstration, as that the whole is bigger than its parts—'and ask me of it, and I can show it in the table, in the window, in a man.' Ironside replied that that was only to demonstrate the attributes of a thing, not

E

the thing in itself, *quod est* and not *quid est*, and that
though such a demonstration was possible in material
objects, it could not apply to the soul, which 'being
insensible was to be discerned by the spirit' and not
by the senses. 'Nothing is more certain in the world
than that there is a god, yet being a spirit to subject
him to the sense otherwise than perfected it is impossible.
Marry, quoth Sir Walter, these two be like for neither
could I learn hitherto what god is.' A Mr Fitzjames
then gave Aristotle's definition, *Ens Entium*, only to be
reproved by Ironside, who said that divinity wanted
not Aristotle to support it: God *was Ens Entium*, whatever Aristotle might say. 'It was most certain, and
confirmed by God himself unto Moses. Yea but what
is *Ens Entium*, saith Sir Walter?' Ironside answered
that it was God. 'And being misliked as before, Sir
Walter wished that grace might be said, for that, quoth
he, is better than this disputation.'[1] Whether this
abrupt conclusion to the dispute was ironical or not is
not altogether clear from the evidence. At any rate,
pestered by spies, next year, in 1595, Ralegh left
England in search of El Dorado.

It is thought that Ralegh's circle is satirized by
Shakespeare in *Love's Labour's Lost*, and that when Berowne
exclaims:

> O paradox! Black is the badge of hell,
> The hue of dungeons and the School of Night.

he is hitting off Ralegh's swarthy complexion, his
atheism, his recent imprisonment and his coterie.
In the person of 'the magnificent Armado,' the fantastic

---

[1] Harleian MSS. 6849, fol. 187. Frances Yates points out that there is a
similarity between Ralegh's behaviour at this supper party and Bruno's as he
pictures it himself in his *Cena de le ceneri* (*A Study of Love's Labour's Lost*, p. 95).

Spaniard, who is a traveller and a dandy, a knight who spends his time writing poetry and long letters to his sovereign about imaginary plots, Miss Bradbrook thinks that Shakespeare intended Ralegh, just as Harriot may be the original of the pedantic schoolmaster Holofernes, whom Don Armado has 'singled from the barbarous' to assist him in the theatricals which are to take place 'in the posteriors of the day, which the vulgar call the afternoon.'[1] If it is Ralegh, the joke is given additional point by making him a Spaniard. Certainly Don Armado's poem is a perfect parody of Ralegh's style:

> Thus dost thou hear the Nemean lion roar
> 'Gainst thee, thou lamb, that standest as his prey:
> Submissive fall his princely feet before,
> And he from forage will incline to play.
> But if thou strive, poor soul, what art thou then?
> Food for his rage, repasture for his den.

There is a parody of *Hero and Leander* in Berowne's speech in praise of love, which otherwise is written quite seriously in Marlowe's manner:

> For valour, is not love a Hercules,
> Sill climbing trees in the Hesperides?

Marlowe had written:

> Leander now like Theban Hercules,
> Enter'd the orchard of the Hesperides.

There is also a very amusing parody of Chapman's grandiloquence:

> The grosser manner of these world's delights
> He throws upon the gross world's baser slaves:
> To love, to wealth, to pomp, I pine and die:
> With all these living in philosophy.

[1] *The School of Night*, pp. 153-69.

Shakespeare, the Johannes Factotum, shows himself here the master of all manners.

Love's Labour's Lost turns, of course, on the notion of the superiority of the school of experience, and particularly the experience of love-making, over the monastic life of learning, extolled by Chapman and Ralegh, in his present melancholy mood of exile from the Court, as the pathway to wisdom. 'Small profit have continual plodders ever got,' says Berowne, 'Save base authority from others' books.' And there is evidently a shrewd hit at Harriot in the lines:

> These country godfathers of heaven's lights
>> That give a name to every fixed star,
> Have no more profit of their shining nights,
>> Than those who walk and wot not what they are.

There are many other contemporary allusions in the play besides those to Ralegh and his circle, pointed out in the New Cambridge edition of *Love's Labour's Lost* and elaborated by Frances Yates and M. C. Bradbrook.

Chapman in 1594 published *The Shadow of Night* and dedicated it to 'My dear and most worthy friend Master Matthew Roydon.' In his prefatory letter, after censuring 'passion-driven men, reading but to curtail a tedious hour,' he recalls in contrast 'how joyfully oftentimes you reported unto me that most ingenious Derby, deep-searching Northumberland, and skill-embracing heir of Hunsdon had most profitably entertained learning in themselves . . . whose high-deserving virtues may cause me hereafter strike that fire out of darkness, which the brightness of day shall envy for beauty.' In his dedication of *Achilles Shield* to 'My admired soul-loved friend, master of all essential and true knowledge, M. Harriot,' he writes that his poetry struggles for birth 'under the claws of this foul panther earth.'

The School of Night's retort to *Love's Labour's Lost* appears to be the mock-serious poem *Willobie his Avisa*, which, for its likeness in style to Roydon's *Elegie, or friend's pastoral for his Astrophill*, Mr G. B. Harrison, in his edition of it, concludes was written by Roydon. We know little of Roydon as a poet, except for Nashe's reference to him in the preface to Greene's *Menaphon*. 'Neither is Spenser the only swallow of our summer,' writes Nash, 'there are extant about London many most able men to revive poetry . . . as namely, Matthew Roydon, Thomas Ache-low, and George Peele; the first of whom, hath showed himself singular in the immortal Epitaph of his beloved Astrophel, besides many other most absolute comic inventions. . . .' *Willobie his Avisa* is certainly a comic invention. 'H. W.,' who may be Henry Wriothesley, Earl of Southampton, is introduced as one of the unsuccessful lovers of Avisa, the virtuous wife of an inn-keeper. For aid in his assault upon Avisa, he turns to 'his familiar friend W. S.,' who is referred to obliquely as an actor and who 'not long before had tried the courtesy of the same passion.' 'W. S.' encour-ages him with a cynical tag:

> She is no saint, she is no nun,
> I think in time she may be won.

which echoes lines from *Titus Andronicus* and *Richard III*. *Willobie his Avisa* was evidently a popular book, for it went into six editions before 1635, which shows, as G. B. Harrison remarks, that it was no hole-in-the-corner affair, but concerned with the private lives of great men. Mr Harrison interprets it, however, as a sequel to Shakespeare's *Rape of Lucrece*, in which many people saw Ralegh the Proud as Tarquin the Ravisher.[1]

By the time he came to write *Hero and Leander*, Marlowe had evidently outgrown the School of Night and was as ready as Shakespeare to laugh at its pretensions. It is all the more curious, therefore, that Chapman should have felt moved by 'strange instigation' to write a continuation of his friend's fragment, which, in its gaiety of temper, is much nearer to *Love's Labour's Lost* than to Chapman's 'soul's dark offspring.'

[1] In an appendix to Mr. Harrison's edition will be found the depositions taken at the Cerne Abbas Commission on Atheism.

Chapter Six

THE SHADOW OF THE STAR CHAMBER

O N 12 May 1593 Thomas Kyd was arrested. His rooms were searched by the police and he himself taken to Bridewell. Tension was increasing in the country. The Spaniards were daily expected to land in the Isle of Man and the plague had assumed the proportions of a national disaster. Meanwhile there were indications of some vast and vaguely defined plot that seemed to be threatening the stability of the whole realm.

The Catholics had been advised to regard the Earl of Derby as one who might, after a general insurrection supported by Spain, be recognized as king in place of the heretic Elizabeth.[1] The authorities were understandably in a state of alarm and redoubled their persecution of both Catholics and Puritans.

In the City, too, there had been vicious outbreaks against foreigners and inflammatory notices were set up on the walls threatening a general rising of the apprentices against the refugee Flemish and the French. 'Be it known,' ran one of these notices, 'to all Flemings

[1] Fernando Stanley, a poet and the patron of poets and of Strange's men, to whom Nashe dedicated his *Piers Penniless* and Chapman his *Shadow of Night*, was approached this year by Richard Hesketh, on behalf of the English Catholics abroad, to set up his claim to the throne and threatened with death if he gave them away. Stanley promptly reported Hesketh to the Privy Council and he was hanged at St. Albans in November. Next April Stanley began to sicken of 'some strange sickness,' says Stowe, and died, in spite of the fact that all through his sickness 'he often took Beza's stone and unicorn's horn.' It was thought that he was bewitched.

and Frenchmen, that it is best for them to depart out
of the realm of England, between this and 9th of July
next. If not, then take what follows. For there shall
be many a sore stripe. Apprentices will rise to the
number of 2,336. And all apprentices and journeymen
will down with Flemings and Strangers.' On 22 April
the Privy Council appointed a commission to investi-
gate the matter. But the libelling continued. On 11
May a libel more threatening and malicious than the
rest appeared on the wall of the Dutch Church and the
Council wrote to the City Corporation that their
commissioners were to take 'extraordinary pains and
care' in examining suspected persons. They were
empowered to search private houses for all manner of
papers and writings that might throw any light upon the
identity of the authors of the libels and suspected
persons were, if necessary, to be tortured for evidence.
Riots in the City were followed by the hanging of four
apprentices on Tower Hill and the carting and whipping
of others. The players, too, were involved. A play of
Sir Thomas More, already in the hands of Sir Edmund
Tilney, Master of the Revels, opened with More paci-
fying a London mob which on 'ill Mayday' 1517 had
attacked the aliens and strangers for eating the bread
of fatherless children—that is, in the language of modern
economists, flooding the English market with cheap
foreign labour. The parallel with the present riots was
too close and Tilney heavily censored the manuscript
of the play, writing across the top of it: 'Leave out
the insurrection wholly and the cause thereof and begin
with Sr. Tho. More at the mayor's sessions with a
report afterwards of his good service done by being
Sheriff of London upon a writing against the Lombards.
Only a short report and not otherwise at your perils.'

The play was then bought from the Admiral's by Strange's men and revised again. That part of the manuscript which is believed to be in Shakespeare's hand makes More rebuke the rioters and arouses sympathy for the foreigners.

In the meantime Kyd's 'waste and idle papers' had been examined and though there was nothing among them which threw any light upon the authors of the libels, the Coucil found something still more dangerous, which they endorsed as 'vile and heretical conceits denying the deity of Jesus Christ.' Being examined under torture, Kyd said that these papers were 'fragments of a disputation' belonging to Marlowe and dated from the time when he and Marlowe were 'writing together in the same room two years since.' They had, he said, got accidentally shuffled among his own papers. As for himself, he assured them, he had no doubts about the deity of Jesus Christ; he abhorred the very idea of atheism, but many people would swear that Marlowe was an atheist. As a matter of fact, the notes in question were a reasoned defence, based on scriptural texts, of the Unitarian or Deist position, though it was for just such opinions that Francis Kett, a fellow of Marlowe's college at Cambridge, had been burnt at Norwich in 1589. They were part of an anonymous treatise quoted by John Proctor, a parish priest of the time of Henry VIII, for confutation in his book *The Fall of the Late Arrian*—Arrian, it is thought, being John Assheton who had denied the doctrine of the Trinity, had been examined by Cramner in 1549 and had recanted. That Marlowe should have had them in his possession is evidence of his continuing preoccupation with theology. The interesting thing about the writer of these fragments is that he quotes 'contraries out of the Scriptures,' a charge which Baines brought against Marlowe. For instance: 'for how may it be thought true religion which uniteth in one subject contraries as visibility and invisibility, mortality and immortality &c. . . . And if Jesus Christ, even he which was born of Mary, was God so shall he be a visible God, comprehensible and mortal, which is not compted God with me quoth great Athanasius of Alexandria &c. For if we be not able to comprehend nor the Angels nor our own souls, which are things create, how wrongfully then and absurdly we make the creator of them comprehensible, especially contrary to so manifest testimonies of the Scriptures &c.'[1] The writer's main point is that if Jesus Christ was subject to human passions and sufferings, as we are told in the New Testament, he cannot be God—a position which Marlowe apparently subscribed to.

We do not know what other charges Kyd brought against Marlowe at this time, but his letters to Puckering written shortly after Marlowe's death may be an expansion of them.[2] His position was particularly precarious, because only Marlowe could prove Kyd's innocence by claiming the papers as his own, and with Marlowe he does not seem to have been just then on very good terms. To Puckering he wrote:

'My first acquaintance with this Marlowe, rose upon his bearing name to serve my Lord, although his Lordship never knew his service, but in writing for his

[1] Harleian MSS. 6848, fols. 187–9. Quoted: F. S. Boas's edition of Kyd's works, pp. cx—cxiii.

[2] Hardin Craig has shown that at least one of the MSS. of the Elizabethan translation of *The Prince* (not printed till 1640) was evidently copied out by Kyd, for the handwriting is the same as in the letters to Puckering. In his preface to Greene's *Menaphon* (1589), Nashe had referred to Kyd as a writer " renouncing all possibility of credit or estimation " by meddling with Italian translations.

players, for never could my Lord endure his name or sight, when he had heard of his conditions, nor would indeed the form of divine prayers used daily in his Lordship's house have quadred with such reprobates.

'That I should be familiar friend with one so irreligious were very rare, when Tully saith *Digni sunt amicitia quibus in ipsis inest causa cur diligantur* which neither was in him, for person, qualities, or honesty, besides he was intemperate and of a cruel heart, the very contraries to which my greatest enemies will say of me.

'It is not to be numbered amongst the best conditions of men to tax or to upbraid the dead, *Quia mortui non mordent*. But thus much have I (with your Lordship's favour) dared in the greatest cause, which is to clear myself of being thought an *Atheist*, which some will swear he was.

'For more assurance that I was not of that vile opinion, let it but please your Lordship to enquire of such as he conversed withal, that is (as I am given to understand) with *Harriot*, *Warner*, *Roydon* and some stationers in Paul's Churchyard, whom I in no sort can accuse nor will excuse by reason of his company; of whose consent if I had been, no question but I also should have been of their consort. . . .'

Asked, perhaps, for further information, Kyd followed this up with another letter in which he set out Marlowe's opinions, as he was accustomed to hear them expressed in his daily conversation.

'First, it was his custom when I knew him first, and as I heard say he continued it in table talk or otherwise, to jest at the divine scriptures, gibe at prayers, and strive in argument to frustrate and confute what hath been spoke or writ by prophets and such holy men.

1. He would report St. John to be Our Saviour Christ's Alexis (I cover it with reverence and trembling) that is, that Christ did love him with an extraordinary love.

2. That for me to write a poem of St. Paul's conversion, as I was determined, he said would be as if I should go write a book of fast and loose, esteeming Paul a juggler.

3. That the prodigal child's portion was but four nobles, he held his purse so near the bottom in all pictures, and that it either was a jest or else four nobles then was thought a great patrimony, not thinking it a proverb.

4. That things esteemed to be done by divine power might have as well been done by observation of men, all which he would so suddenly take slight occasions to slip out as I and many others, in regard of his other rashness in attempting sudden privy injuries to men did overslip though often reprehend him for it, and for which God is my witness as well by my Lord's commandment, as in hatred of his life and thoughts I left and did refrain his company.

'He would persuade with men of quality to go unto the King of Scots, whither I hear *Roydon* is gone and where, if he had lived, he told me, when I saw him last, he meant to be.'

The first thing to be noticed about these charges is that they ring true. They are, in fact, the sort of thing we should expect from the author of *Tamburlaine* and *The Jew of Malta*. Moreover, they are supported, sometimes almost word for word, by the independent testimony of other witnesses. It appears that when Marlowe was contradicted he lost his temper and resorted to violence, also that he was in intimate contact with men of quality. The charge that he intended 'to go unto the King of Scots' is not so treasonable as it appears at first sight, though certainly dangerous. Evidently Marlowe thought that James VI of Scotland was to succeed Elizabeth and he may have planned to ingratiate himself with the new king in good time, for James's favour to learned men was well known.

As a result of Kyd's confessions and 'the vile and heretical conceits,' on 18 May a warrant was issued to Henry Maunder, 'one of the Messengers of her Majesty's Chamber, to repair to the house of Mr. Walsingham in Kent, or to any other place where he shall understand Christopher Marlowe to be remaining, and by virtue thereof to apprehend him and bring him to the Court in his company. And in case of need to require aid.'

Aid was not required and Marlowe replied to the summons promptly. Two days later it is recorded that 'Christopher Marley of London, gentlemen, being sent for by warrant from their Lordships, hath entered his appearance accordingly for his indemnity therein, and is commanded to give his daily attendance on their Lordships until he shall be licensed to the contrary.'[1]

Marlowe appears to have been treated with courtesy and consideration by the Privy Council. He was merely required to be at hand as a witness, or until such time as the Council had accummulated further evidence against him, which they now proceeded to do. His prompt answer to their summons and the fact that he was staying with Thomas Walsingham evidently stood in his favour. Possibly, too, on turning up the file marked 'Marlowe' their lordships remembered his 'good and faithful dealing.'

[1] *Acts of the Privy Council*, edited by J. R. Dasent, xxiv, 244.

The Council's enquiries about Marlowe resulted in the delivery towards the end of the month by the informer Richard Baines of such a horrifying list of blasphemies and other accusations that a copy of them was sent to the Queen. Unfortunately we do not know exactly when Baines handed in his *Note containing the opinion of one Christopher Marly concerning his damnable judgement of religion and scorn of God's Word*, for the document is undated. But the copy sent to the Queen is headed: 'A Note delivered on Whitsun eve last of the most horrible blasphemies uttered by Christopher Marly who within iii days after came to a sudden and fearful end of his life.' Whitsun eve in 1593 fell on 2 June and by that time Marlowe had been dead for two days. So the scribe made a mistake either in the date of the delivery of the *Note* or in the date of Marlowe's death. If Baines delivered the *Note* on Whitsun eve, he evidently knew nothing of Marlowe's death a few days before, for he concludes: 'I think all men in Christianity ought to endeavour that the mouth of so dangerous a member may be stopped.' If he was busily employed collecting information against Marlowe during the second half of May, it seems most peculiar that he should not have known about Marlowe's death, had it already occurred. In fact, it looks as though Baines really did deliver his report three days before Marlowe was killed.

According to this report, Marlowe was in the habit of saying:

'That the Indians and many authors of antiquity have assuredly written above sixteen thousand years agone, whereas Adam is proved to have lived within six thousand years.

'He affirmeth that Moses was but a juggler, and that

one Heriots [Harriot], being Sir Walter Ralegh's man, can do more than he.

'That Moses made the Jews to travel 40 years in the wilderness, which journey might have been done in less than one year, ere they came to the promised land, to the intent that those who were privy to most of his subtleties might perish, and so an everlasting superstition remain in the hearts of the people.

'That the first beginning of religion was only to keep men in awe.

'That it was an easy matter for Moses, being brought up in all the arts of the Egyptians, to abuse the Jews, being a rude and gross people.

'That Christ was a bastard and His mother dishonest.

'That He was the son of a carpenter, and that if the Jews among whom He was born did crucify Him they best knew Him and whence He came.

'That Christ deserved better to die than Barabbas, and that the Jews made a good choice, though Barabbas were both a thief and a murderer.

'That if there be any God or any good religion, then it is in the papists, because the service of God is performed with more ceremonies, as elevation of the Mass, organs, singing men, shaven crowns &c. That all Protestants are hypocritical asses.

'That if he were put to write a new religion, he would undertake both a more excellent and admirable method, and that the New Testement is filthily written.

'That the woman of Samaria and her sister were whores and that Christ knew them dishonestly.

'That St. John the Evangelist was bedfellow to Christ and leaned always in his bosom; that he used him as the sinners of Sodoma.

'That all they that love not tobacco and boys were fools.

'That all the apostles were fishermen and base fellows neither of wit nor worth; that Paul only had wit but he was a timorous fellow in bidding men to be subject to magistrates against his conscience.

'That he had as good right to coin as the Queen of England, and that he was acquainted with one Poole, a prisoner in Newgate, who hath great skill in mixture of metals; and having learned such things of him, he meant, through the help of a cunning stamp-maker, to coin French crowns, pistolets and English shillings.

'That if Christ would have instituted the sacrament with more ceremonial reverence it would have been had in more admiration; that it would have been much better being administered in a tobacco pipe.

'That the Angel Gabriel was bawd to the Holy Ghost, because he brought the salutation to Mary.

'That one Richard Cholmley hath confessed that he was persuaded by Marlowe's reasons to become an atheist.

'These things, with many other, shall by good and honest witness be approved to be his opinions and common speeches; and that this Marlowe doth not only hold them himself, but almost into every company he cometh he persuadeth men to atheism, willing them not to be afeard of bugbears and hobgoblins, and utterly scorning both God and His ministers, as I, Richard Baines, will justify and approve, both by mine oath and the testimony of many honest men; and almost all men with whom he hath conversed at any time will testify the same; and, as I think, all men in Christianity ought to endeavour that the mouth of so dangerous a member may be stopped. He saith likewise that he hath quoted a number of contrarieties out of the Scripture, which he hath given to some great men who in convenient time shall be named. When these things shall be called in question the witness shall be produced.—Richard Baines.'[1]

This document is usually referred to as 'the Baines libel,' but there is no reason why its charges should not have been perfectly true. They are not the sort of things that sound as though they could have been made up, any more than Kyd's charges. Further, they are substantiated by the independent reports contained in *Remembrances of words and matter against Richard Cholmeley*, who is evidently echoing Marlowe. In both the Baines *Note* and the *Remembrances* against Chomley, Marlowe's name is linked with Ralegh's, and that Baines is not making idle charges is shown by his willingness to produce witnesses and even to implicate 'some great men who in convenient time shall be named.'

The opinions here attributed to Marlowe would be startling enough in any age; in his own they show an almost incredible rashness. Some of them are merely lewd, schoolboyish blasphemies, but others plainly spring from the close reasoning of the one-time theological student.[2] Most of them show a trenchant sense of humour—especially the paragraph about Moses and the Jews in the wilderness.

It has been argued that Baines's *Note* is made up of sentences taken at random from the actual 'atheist lecture' which Marlowe is reported to have read to Ralegh and that here we have extracts from that lost

---

[1] Harleian MSS. 6848, ff. 185–6.

[2] 'Marlowe, the most thoughtful, the most blasphemous (and therefore, probably, the most Christian) of his contemporaries . . .' writes T. S. Eliot in 'Shakespeare and the Stoicism of Seneca.'

F

'book against the Trinity' which Thomas Beard mentions. Beard also refers to his views about Moses and Christ and reports him as saying that all religion is 'but a device of policy.' He also mentions his blasphemous conversation. We must conclude, therefore, that Baines's *Note* is rather a true report than a libel, certainly not a forgery as J. H. Ingram contended in his *Christopher Marlowe and his Associates*.

Beyond the fact that Ralegh's and Harriot's names are mentioned, the *Note* provides further evidence of Marlowe's association with Ralegh's circle at Sherborne, because some of the opinions resemble the findings of the Cerne Abbas Commission on Atheism of 1594. A small, but significant, point is the emphasis on tobacco pipes and smoking, a practice which at this time was still confined to Ralegh's immediate circle. Coupled with smoking, is the plea for 'buggery' which was, of course, a capital offence under Elizabethan law. But any one of the more blasphemous accusations, supported by witnesses, would have been sufficient to condemn Marlowe to death, probably at the stake. To most of his contemporaries his opinions must have seemed utterly devilish and terrifying—as they were doubtless intended to be. A man who thought and talked in this way, they must have felt, would be capable of anything and was, indeed, hardly human. In the *Spaccio*, Giordano Bruno had referred to Moses and Aaron as jugglers, to the existence of men before Adam, whose 'Memories and Records of about 10,000 years are still entire and round.' He was arrested by the Holy Office in Venice just a year before the Privy Council sent for Marlowe. Among the opinions attributed to him by Mocenigo in May 1592—opinions which he denied at his trial— were such blasphemies as 'that Christ was a paltry wretch; that since he worked evil to lead away the people, he might very well foretell he would be hanged; that Christ worked miracles in appearance only and that he was a magician and the Apostles also, and that he (Bruno) could do as much and more.' It was also alleged that he denied the sacraments and made jokes about the Last Judgement. The parallel with Marlowe's case is so close that it is clear where many of his opinions came from.

Additional support of the charges of both Baines and Kyd appears in Lodge's *Wits Misery* (1596) where, describing the character Derision, who otherwise bears some resemblance to Marlowe, he says that he is one 'whose meerest profession is Atheism. . . . Christ his Saviour a carpenter's son . . . such blasphemy he uttereth betwixt the Holy Ghost and the Blessed and Immaculate Virgin Mary as my heart trembleth to think them and my tongue abhorreth to speak them.'

Chapter Seven

DEPTFORD STRAND

A T ten o'clock in the morning of 30 May 1593 four gentlemen met together at the house of a certain Eleanor Bull, widow, on Deptford Green. They were Christopher Marlowe, Robert Poley, Ingram Frizer and Nicholas Skeres. All four had a common acquaintance in Thomas Walsingham of Scadbury. Three of them had worked in the secret service as spies and messengers. In fact, Poley had only that morning returned from abroad, carrying 'letters in post for her Majesty's special and secret affairs of great importance.' Officially, he was on his way to the Court at Nonesuch, but he did not deliver his despatches until 8 June, though he is described as being all this while in the Queen's service. Skeres had worked in conjunction with him during the Babington Plot; earlier, in 1582, Skeres was associated with Marlowe's friend Matthew Roydon of Thavies Inn in a bond for the repayment of a debt to a London goldsmith, in which he is described as of Furnival's Inn. In the summer of 1593 Skeres and Frizer were occupied in the swindling of young Drew Woodleff, proceedings from which Thomas Walsingham also apparently benefited, for Frizer was then acting as his business agent.

According to the best informed contemporary account, that by William Vaughan in *The Golden Grove*, it was Frizer who invited Marlowe 'to a feast' at Deptford. Professor Boas remarks that 'there is a suspicious resemblance between the setting of the Deptford episode and an incident in the Babington conspiracy, when a number of plotters . . . might have been taken "at supper" in Poley's garden, probably the Garden Inn in Fleet Street.'

Certainly Poley's suppers proved to be last suppers for a good many people and Jonson, in his epigram 'Inviting a Friend to Supper,' declares: 'And we will have no Pooley or Parrott by . . .' But as Poley had only just returned from abroad, the party could hardly have been arranged by him. It is more likely that Marlowe and Skeres had come to meet him at Deptford on his return, invited by Ingram Frizer.

Whatever construction we may care to give this meeting—and there is nothing very strange or mysterious about it, as all four men were known to each other already—Marlowe, Frizer, Poley and Skeres dined early in a private room and after dinner were 'in quiet sort together' and walked in the garden of the house 'until the sixth hour after noon.'

About six in the evening, they left the garden and went indoors to supper. After supper, Marlowe lay down on a bed, while Poley, Frizer and Skeres sat playing backgammon at a table near the bed, but with their backs to it. As they were playing, an argument arose between Marlowe and Frizer about the bill—'le recknynge,' as it is called in the Coroner's report. The argument became so heated that Marlowe suddenly sprang up, drew Frizer's dagger, which was hanging at his belt, and dealt him two or three cuts across the head with it. Probably, as has been suggested, he pommelled Frizer's head with the hilt of the dagger, as was customary among Elizabethans before beginning to fight in earnest.[1] Frizer, who was sitting on a bench between Poley and Skeres, with his legs wedged under the table, in such a position that he could not get up to defend himself, struggled to get back his dagger. In this struggle the point was driven into Marlowe's skull, just over the right eye, inflicting a wound two inches deep of which, we are told, he instantly died.

There is really nothing improbable about this story. If Marlowe was pommelling Frizer's head with the hilt of the dagger, this would leave the blade pointing backwards, so that when Frizer turned and seized his wrist, in an effort to get the dagger away from him, it is quite likely that the point would be driven backwards and upwards into Marlowe's face. Whether a blow inflicted in this way would be of sufficient force to penetrate the skull, is another matter. We are told, on medical evidence, that a wound two inches deep above the eye, such as Frizer is said to have inflicted, would not have caused instant death, but would have resulted in a state of coma lasting several days.[2] Nor is it mentioned in the Coroner's report that Poley and Skeres tried to intervene. Evidently everything was over before they had time to bestir themselves.

Such, at any rate, was the evidence that satisfied a Middlesex jury at the inquest two days later. It was presided over by William Danby, the Coroner of the Queen's Household, because Marlowe's death had occurred 'within the verge'——that is, within twelve miles of the sovereign's person. 'Christopher Morley's' body was viewed by a jury of whom eleven have since

[1] William Poel, The Death of Marlowe, *Times Literary Supplement*, 21 May, 1925.

[2] S. A. Tannenbaum, *The Assassination of Christopher Marlowe.*

been identified through their wills.[1] These were: Nicholas Draper, gentleman; Wolstan Randall, gentleman; William Curry, gentleman; John Barber of Chatham, carpenter; Robert Baldwyn, of East Greenwich, yeoman; Giles Field, of Deptford, grocer; George Halfpenny, of Limehouse, baker; James Batt, of Lewisham, husbandman; Thomas Batt, senior, of Bromley Kent, yeoman; Henry Awger, a manorial tenant; and Henry Dabyns (Dobbins), baker. There is no reason to suppose that these men were either suborned, as has been suggested, or particularly stupid. Most of them had probably never heard of Marlowe before. They went about their duties in a business-like way, reconstructing the quarrel, its cause and effects, measuring the wound over the corpse's right eye and valuing the dagger that caused it at a shilling. After weighing the evidence, they concluded that Frizer had killed Marlowe in self-defence.

And that is all we know. Unfortunately the individual depositions of Frizer, Poley and Skeres have not been preserved. Again, so far as is known, the jury relied solely on the evidence of these three men—two of them swindlers and the other a self-confessed perjurer. 'I will swear and forswear myself,' Poley told Yeomans— the husband of the girl with whom he was having an affair in prison, 'rather than I will accuse myself to do me any harm.' Poley was telling Yeomans about his cross-examination by Sir Francis Walsingham as to his having in his possession a copy of the proscribed *Leicester's Commonwealth*, and on this occasion, he said, he had 'put Mr. Secretary into that heat that he looked out his window and grinned like a dog.' It is open to

---

[1] E. Vine Hall, *Testamentary Papers III* and J. W. Kirby, *Times Literary Supplement*, 17 July, 1930.

us to believe, of course, that a man who was too clever
for Francis Walsingham, the head of the secret service,
would certainly be too good for an innocent jury of
bakers, carpenters, farmers and grocers, with a sprink-
ling of local gentry.

But there is really no evidence for supposing that
the story of Marlowe's death was concocted. Taking
into account what Kyd called 'his other rashness in
attempting sudden privy injuries to men,' it is more
than likely that this is how he would behave in such a
situation. Probably they had all been drinking, and,
although they had apparently relaxed for the moment,
all four men had been in conference together since ten
o'clock in the morning. With his impending examination
by the Privy Council, there was every reason for
Marlowe to be on edge. He may have met his friends
at Deptford for the purpose of discussing the best
attitude to adopt at this examination, or the best way
of avoiding it altogether by escaping to Scotland. Kyd,
it will be remembered, told Puckering later that, the
last time they met, Marlowe had expressed his intention
of following Roydon's example and going to Scotland.
If he was really thinking of that line of escape, Poley
was the very man to help him to it.

At any rate, Shakespeare seems to have accepted
the story of his death as it came out at the inquest, for
in *As You Like It* Touchstone remarks: 'When a man's
verses cannot be understood nor a man's good wit
seconded with the forward child Understanding, it
strikes a man more dead than a great reckoning in a
little room.' Since Marlowe, Frizer, Poley and Skeres
had been spending all day at Eleanor Bull's tavern, the
reckoning was most likely a large one. Touchstone's
cryptic remark is followed almost immediately by a

direct quotation from *Hero and Leander*, when Phoebe, addressing Marlowe's shade, says:

> Dead Shepherd, now I find thy saw of might:
> 'Who ever lov'd that lov'd not at first sight?'

It is usually the clowns who make topical allusions in Elizabethan drama and it was Marlowe's 'good wit' that got him so many enemies. Shakespeare must have been haunted by the miserable death of his great rival, and when in the *Sonnets* he is thinking of his own possible death from 'the coward conquest of a wretch's knife' he must have thought of it again.

It is a thousand pities that Nashe's elegy 'On Marlowe's Untimely Death' is lost, though he refers to him in *Christ's Tears Over Jerusalem*, which was entered in the Stationers' Register on 8 September of this year, as 'poor deceased Kit Marlowe.' Chapman, who, one might think, would have been repelled by Marlowe's opinions and general conversation, if it really was as blasphemous as reported, wrote, in his continuation of *Hero and Leander*, of

> his free soul, whose living subject stood
> Up to the chin in the Pierian flood.

Peele in *The Honour of the Garter* refers to him as 'Marley, the Muses' darling,' in close association with Watson; Drayton writes of the divine rapture of his poetry, and Henry Petoe tells us that *Hero and Leander*

> moved such delight,
> That men would shun their sleep in still dark night
> To meditate upon his golden lines.

Dr. Tannenbaum has argued that Marlowe was assassinated at the instigation of Ralegh, who feared to be implicated still further when the time came for Marlowe to be examined by the Privy Council. It has also been supposed that Frizer, Poley and Skeres were the hired assassins of the Privy Council itself. But there is no reason why the Privy Council should have employed such a hole-in-the-corner method of getting rid of Marlowe, and had Ralegh employed Frizer, Poley and Skeres to murder him he would have been putting his life entirely in their hands. It is true that Ralegh's name was removed from the copy of the Baines *Note* sent to the Queen, and Dr. Tannenbaum thinks that the same influences that contrived this also contrived to shut Marlowe's mouth for good and all. Both these arguments rest on the assumption that the story of his death was faked and that the Coroner had been advised not to inquire too closely into its circumstances.

But there is really no need for all this elaborate speculation. An Elizabethan jury would not see anything suspicious in such a common occurrence as a tavern brawl. 'Le recknyng' has been the cause of many disagreements, before and since, and at a time when men wore swords and daggers, and used them freely, such disputes were apt to have a fatal ending.

Marlowe was buried immediately after the inquest in the old churchyard of St. Nicholas, Deptford. No stone marks his grave, but the church register records the burial under Anno Dom. 1593 as: 'Christopher Marlow, slaine by ffrancis ffrezer; the 1. of June.' A pardon was issued to Frizer on 28 June on the ground that he had killed Marlowe in defence of his own life.

The day after the issue of this pardon, Frizer was conducting business for Thomas Walsingham. In June 1598 Ann Woodleff of Aylesbury, Bucks, and her son Drew complained to the Lord Keeper about these proceedings of 'about five years now past.' Woodleff had originally appealed to Skeres for a loan to pay off his debts. Skeres introduced him to Frizer, who got him to sign a bond for £60 and instead of cash persuaded him to accept some guns on Tower Hill. When Woodleff asked for the guns to be converted into cash, Frizer brought him £30 with the story that that was all he had been able to get for them. As if this was not sufficient indication of Frizer's business methods, Woodleff then signed another bond in favour of Frizer for twenty marks. When these bonds fell due Woodleff was unable to meet them, so Frizer induced him to enter 'into a statute for £200 unto a gentleman of good worship . . ., the said Frizer his then Master.' It has since appeared that on 29 June 1593 'Drew Woodleff of Peterley, Bucks, gentleman,' was bound to Thomas Walsingham of Chislehurst, Kent, in the sum of £200 to be paid by 25 July 1593. Woodleff also defaulted on this payment and the case went to Chancery. Meanwhile the Woodleffs had sold Frizer two houses and thirty acres of land, which he promptly resold. He was able to wriggle out of the Woodleffs' charges in 1598 on the plea that they were outlaws. He went to live at Eltham, where Thomas Walsingham, who had been knighted by Elizabeth in 1597, was keeper of the royal park. After that it is Lady Audrey Walsingham with whom Frizer is principally associated. Lady Audrey seems to have been engaged in political intrigue of some sort, though she enjoyed high favour with the Queen, who made her a lady of the bedchamber and gave her purses of money. From Cecil she received the estate of a dispossessed Catholic. She continued to enjoy royal favour under James I, and on 28 December 1604 the king granted a lease of land to Ingram Frizer for her use. Subsequently Frizer negotiated several other leases of royal land in her favour. In fact Lady Audrey stood so high in the esteem of James I that it has been supposed that her political intrigues must have been connected with his accession to the English throne. From all of this it begins to look as though Marlowe's talk of 'going unto the King of Scots,' to which course he would 'persuade men of quality,' may have had its origin at Scadbury. This gives us another possible clue to his death, suggested by Bakeless: namely, that it was Audrey Walsingham who feared the result of his examination by the Privy Council and employed Frizer, her agent, to put him out of the way before he could repeat the treasonable talk he had overheard at Scadbury.

Francis Meres, writing in 1598, tells us in _Palladis Tamia_ that Marlowe was killed by a rival in love: 'Christofer Marlow was stabbed to death by a bawdy serving man, a rival of his in his lewd love.' This story is repeated by Anthony à Wood in the next century, who writes in his _Athenae Oxonienses_—'He being deeply in love with a certain woman, had for his rival a bawdy serving-man, . . .' If so, we may, if we like, imagine both Marlowe and Frizer in love with Lady Audrey. Certainly Marlowe had been living in her husband's house. A tenuous clue in support of this theory may be found in the so-called Thornborough Commonplace Book, now in the Folger Shakespeare Library at Washington. This book contains a manuscript version of Marlowe's lyric _Come Live with Me and be My Love_. It had belonged to Mrs. John Thornborough of Bristol, and Lady Audrey Walsingham is named as one of her friends.[1] Perhaps, suggests Bakeless, the book had originally belonged to Lady Audrey.

[1] Bakeless, _The Tragicall History of Christopher Marlowe_, I. 166.

Of the survivors of the Deptford tragedy, Ingram Frizer died in 1627 having been churchwarden at Eltham since 1603. Poley continued in his government service as messenger and spy till the end of the century. Skeres was put to spy, it seems, on the Earl of Essex, but was arrested in March 1595 'in very dangerous company' at the house of one Williamson, when he is described as 'Nicholas Kyrse, alias Skeers, servant of the Earl of Essex.' He was imprisoned in the Counter in Wood Street. In 1601 the Council issued a warrant to the keeper of the prison of Newgate for the removal of 'Nicholas Skiers' into Bridewell. Richard Baines was hanged at Tyburn on 6 December 1594, and Kyd, Marlowe's other accuser, died in the same year, 'worn out and utterly broken by his bitter times and privy passions.'

The miserable death of so famous an 'atheist' and 'filthy playmaker' as Marlowe was hailed exultantly by the Puritan pamphleteers as a manifest sign of divine retribution. Thomas Beard, writing four years after the event and evidently drawing upon contemporary gossip, relates, in his *Theatre of God's Judgements*, that 'one of our own nation, of fresh and late memory, called Marlin . . . denied God and his son Christ, and not only in word blasphemed the Trinity, but also (as it is credibly reported) wrote a book against it, affirming our Saviour to be a deceiver, and Moses to be but a conjurer and seducer of the people, and the Holy Bible to be but vain and idle stories, and all religion but a device of policy.' All of which bears out the earlier charges of Baines. He adds that Marlowe's death occurred in 'London streets' which may, as Hotson has suggested, be a printer's error for 'London streete,' a thoroughfare in East Greenwich, Deptford being West Greenwich. He also knew that in the death struggle Marlowe and his adversary made use of the same dagger. 'As he purposed to stab one whom he ought a grudge unto with his dagger, the other party, perceiving, so avoided the stroke that withal catching hold of his wrist, he stabbed his own dagger into his own head, in such sort, that notwithstanding all the means of surgery that could be wrought, he shortly after died thereof. The manner of his death being so terrible (for he even cursed and blasphemed to his last gasp) and together with his breath an oath flew out of his mouth, that it was not only a manifest sign of God's judgement, but an horrible and fearful terror to all that beheld him. But herein did the justice of God most notably appear, in that he compelled his own hand which had written those blasphemies, to be the instrument to punish him and that in the brain, which had devised the same.'

Apart from its religious tendentiousness, Beard's account is remarkably circumstantial. There is no mention in the inquest proceedings of 'all the means of surgery' having been tried to save Marlowe's life, but if Marlowe did not die 'instantly' from his wound he may have died in agony and if so it was natural that he should die swearing. William Vaughan, in his *Golden Grove* (1600), gives a slightly different account, but one founded on evidently independent information. He gets the name of the place right ('at Detford, a little village about three miles distant from London') and says that when Marlowe was about to stab 'one named Ingram, that had invited him thither to a feast, and was then playing at tables, he quickly perceiving it, so avoided the thrust, that withal drawing out his dagger for his defence he stabbed this Marlowe into the eye . . .' Neither account suggests that Marlowe's death arose out of anything but a personal quarrel, though neither mentions the bill as the cause of it, and Vaughan calls Frizer by his Christian name, as in the Coroner's inquisition and the Queen's pardon, where he appears as 'the said Ingram' and 'the same Ingram.' Both Beard's and Vaughan's accounts are of value as showing how Marlowe's death was regarded by the religious pamphleteers. It is a pity that his fellow poets were so silent about it. The best epitaph was written by Michael Drayton:

> Next Marlowe, bathed in the Thespian springs,
> Had in him those brave translunary things
> That your first poets had; his raptures were
> All air and fire, which made his verses clear,
> For that fine madness still he did retain,
> Which rightly should possess a poet's brain.
> *Of Poets and Poesie*

It was not till 1891 that a memorial was erected to Marlowe's memory at Canterbury, when Henry Irving unveiled a monument in the Butter Market designed by that genteel Victorian sculptor Onslow Ford to represent the chief characters of the plays. In 1921 it was moved to the Dane John, and unveiled on this new site in 1928 by Hugh Walpole, also an old King's schoolboy. In 1919 an unknown admirer put up a brass plate in St. Nicholas, Deptford, 'To the Immortal Memory of Christopher Marlowe M.A. The Founder of Grandiloquent Blank Verse.' From the correspondence dealing with the erection of the 1891 memorial we learn that it was not thought fitting that Marlowe should be commemorated in Westminster Abbey, in view of his 'acknowledged life and expressions.'

Chapter Eight

DRAMA

(i) DIDO, QUEEN OF CARTHAGE

Written 1586–7, revised 1592–3.

Published 1594 by the widow Orwin for Thomas Woodcock at the Sign of the Black Bear in Paul's Churchyard.

Stage History. Acted at an unspecified date by the Children of the Chapel Royal. Possibly the same *Dido* as that acted by Admiral's men at Henslowe's Rose on 8 January 1596, and the same 'tragedy of Aeneas and Dido' as seen by the French Ambassador, M. de la Boderie, at an entertainment given before James I in June 1607.

Source. The first, second and fourth books of the *Aeneid*, Ovid's *Metamorphoses*.

Plot. Aeneas, escaping from the sack of Troy, is wrecked on the coast of Libya and throws himself upon the mercy of Dido, Queen of Carthage. Venus, his mother, assures him of her protection. She transforms Ascanius, Aeneas's small son, into the semblance of Cupid. Dido, dandling Cupid-Ascanius, is pricked in the breast by him and falls in love with Aeneas, though she has previously pledged herself to Iarbus. Iarbus is loved by Anna, Dido's sister. As a token of her love, Dido refits the Trojan fleet. During a storm, which overtakes the royal hunting party, Dido confesses her love to Aeneas. Mercury appears to Aeneas and tells him that he must leave Dido and Carthage in order to found Rome. When Aeneas after one unsuccessful attempt, finally leaves, Dido throws herself into the flames of a funeral pyre, Anna follows her and Iarbus kills himself in despair.

THE play is clearly written with a juvenile company in view. Though an immature work, it is important for the student of Marlowe because it contains all the most characteristic elements of his verse in their earliest form. It is the only play of Marlowe's in which sexual love is the motive-force of the action and thus the only one which gives extended portraits of women. Some parts of it are a line for line translation of Virgil, but others show a highly imaginative handling of his source, particularly Aeneas's famous narration of the sack of Troy, where the verse suddenly leaps from prettiness to greatness.

> Then he unlock'd the horse, and suddenly
> From out his entrails, Neoptolemus
> Setting his spear upon the ground, leapt forth,
> And after him a thousand Grecians more,
> In whose stern faces shin'd the quenchless fire
> That after burnt the pride of Asia.

Marlowe fills out Virgil's matter-of-fact account with many lurid details. The effect of such a line as 'We saw Cassandra sprawling in the streets' creates an atmosphere of nightmare horror, which is heightened by touches of the grotesque. It is a style which achieves its effect, as T. S. Eliot has remarked, by stopping just short of caricature. The passage beginning,

> At last came Pyrrhus fell and full of ire,
> His harness dropping blood, and on his spear
> The mangled head of Priam's youngest son,
> And after him his band of myrmidons,
> With balls of wildfire in their murdering paws . . .

G

was evidently in Shakespeare's mind when Hamlet asks the players to rehearse old Priam's slaughter in the play which was 'caviare to the general.' 'One speech I chiefly loved,' he says, ''twas Aeneas' tale to Dido, and thereabout of it especially where he speaks of Priam's slaughter.'

Dido appears to have been begun at Cambridge, during Marlowe's undergraduate years, for the greater number of the parallels of thought and wording are with the Ovid translation and *Tamburlaine*. But there are also parallels with *Edward II* and *Hero and Leander*, which suggest that he took it up again and revised it in later life. Though Nashe's name follows Marlowe's on the title page in smaller type, there are few discernible traces of his handiwork, which may have been confined to preparing the play for the press. Both Bishop Tanner and Warton declare that an elegy on Marlowe's death by Nashe was inserted in copies of the 1594 edition seen by them in the eighteenth century, but all traces of this elegy have now disappeared.

As it stands, *Dido* presents a queer mixture of verse styles, swinging from the preciousness of

> Her silver arms will coll me round about,
> And tears of pearl cry, 'Stay, Aeneas, stay!'

to the vigour of

> if thou wilt stay,
> Leap in mine arms; mine arms are open wide:
> If not, turn from me, and I'll turn from thee . . .

Already a key word of Marlowe's imagery is 'crystal,' as when Aeneas is planning to build new walls for Carthage:

> And clad her in a crystal livery,
> Wherein the day may evermore delight.

Certain lines were incorporated in *Tamburlaine*, where they are less effective than in their original context. As a whole the play is little more than a charming piece, suitable for presentation by children, but there are moments, particularly in the scenes between Dido and Aeneas, and between Anna and Iarbus, where real passion breaks through the decorative mould. *Dido* belongs to the graceful genre of Peele's *David and Bethsabe*, a genre which was too small to contain Marlowe's fiery spirit for long.

(ii) TAMBURLAINE THE GREAT

Written 1587.

Published 1590 by Richard Jones at the sign of the Rose and Crown near Holborn Bridge. There is a copy of this edition in the Bodleian Library and another in the Huntington Library. A copy of the second edition of 1593 is in the British Museum.

Stage History. First acted by the Lord Admiral's men 'upon stages in the city of London.' A letter from Philip Gawdy to his father of 16 November 1587 mentions an accident which occurred when the Admiral's men tied one of their fellows to a post and shot him to death. This is usually accepted as a reference to the death of the Governor of Babylon, which occurs in *Tamburlaine Part II*. Robert Greene refers in the preface to *Perimedes* (1588) to Marlowe 'daring God out of his heaven with that atheist Tamburlan.' Tamburlaine was one of Edward Alleyn's greatest roles, and the play was frequently performed by the Admiral's men at Henslowe's Rose during the 1590's.

Sources. George Whetstone's *The English Mirror*, Perondinus's *Magni Tamerlanis Scythiarum Imperatoris Vita* (Florence, 1553), Lonicerus's *Chronicorum Turcicorum*, Abraham Ortelius's atlas *Theatrum Orbis Terrarum*, and Paul Ive's *Practise of Fortification*.

Plot. Mycetes, King of Persia, sends his general Theridamas to put down a petty Turkoman chieftain, Tamburlaine. Theridamas is bewitched by Tamburlaine's visions of world conquest and by the splendour of his person and becomes his follower. Tamburlaine encourages Cosroe to depose his brother Mycetes. He then takes from Cosroe both his crown and his life. He falls in love with Zenocrate, the captured daughter of the Soldan of Egypt, and overcomes Bajazeth, the Great Turk, whom he shuts up in a cage like a wild beast. Tamburlaine announces that he is the appointed Scourge of God and terror of the world. Bajazeth and Zabina, his wife, dash their brains out against the bars of their cage. Part I ends with the sack of Damascus and the slaughter of the virgins, which prepares the way for Tamburlaine's marriage to Zenocrate.

In Part II Tamburlaine's conquests are extended, and his lust for power becomes a mania. He pays the penalty for his blasphemy and defiance of the gods by madness, by the death of Zenocrate and finally by his own death. The high spot of the play is the entrance of Tamburlaine in a chariot drawn by the conquered kings, bitted and bridled like horses. An incident from Hungarian history is introduced in order to show the faithlessness of the Christians, when Sigismund breaks his oath to Orcanes. The capture of Babylon is the signal for a general slaughter. Tamburlaine burns the Koran and challenges Mahomet to avenge the slaughter of the faithful. Shortly after this he begins to sicken and dies. *Tamburlaine Part II* is, therefore, in the nature of a divine retribution for *hubris*.

Tamburlaine, as Marlowe conceived him, illustrates the victory of the imagination over the material world, the heroic will that transcends human limitations and aspires to the divine. Again and again, he is compared to the sun in glory. He is the 'chiefest lamp of the earth' and has his 'rising in the east.' He 'rides in golden armour like the sun' and challenges the power of Jove.

The whole of the first part of *Tamburlaine* is bathed in
the golden, ethereal glow of the conqueror's semi-
divine aspiration and pride of life.[1]

In contradistinction to the active principle of Tamburlaine, the contemplative imagination is embodied
in Zenocrate, who is clad in the cold beauty of the
moon. Instead of the ruddy-gold splendours of the sun
god, Zenocrate appears

> . . . lovelier than the love of Jove,
> Brighter than is the silver Rhodope,
> Fairer than whitest snow on Scythian hills. . . .

She is drawn through frozen regions by milk-white
harts upon an ivory sledge; she scales 'the icy mountains
lofty tops'; she is 'the world's fair eye'; her looks clear
the air with crystal and she is clad in light shed from

> The shining bower where Cynthia sits
> Like lovely Thetis in a crystal robe.

To Tamburlaine she is the symbol of all the immaterial,
unattainable loveliness that flies beyond his reach. In
the second part of the play his is the fury of destruction
of a man who can never possess the ideal beauty conceived by his imagination. It is a beauty clear, crystalline
and remote, the same with which Helen of Troy is
invested in *Doctor Faustus* and which also distinguishes
the E Flat Major Symphony of Mozart—'a transparent
veil for a power which is not physical.'[2] For Zenocrate,
Tamburlaine has the same kind of mystical beauty.

[1] There would seem to be a definite Mithraic element in Marlowe's conception of Tamburlaine. Mithra was the god of battles and also the sun-god
and, as such, his cult was a powerful rival to Christianity under the later
Roman Empire.

[2] M. C. Bradbrook, *The School of Night*, p. 112–6.

As looks the Sun through Nilus' flowing stream,
Or when the morning holds him in her arms,
So looks my lordly love, fair Tamburlaine. . . .

To Marlowe's contemporaries, Tamburlaine con-
formed to the idea of the choleric man—fiery in spirit,
prone to anger, scorn and mockery. The choleric
humour is hot and dry and, if uncontrolled, consumes
both the heart and the brain.[1] Excessive in all things,
elemental, Tamburlaine has few human attributes and
is, therefore, scarcely measurable by human standards.
True to his aspiring character, he bases his right to
betray his ally Cosroe, and supersede him as King of
Persia, on the example of Jove, who was moved by
'The thirst of reign and sweetness of a crown To thrust
his doting father from his chair.' And Tamburlaine
cries

What better precedent than mighty Jove?
Nature that fram'd us of four elements,
Warring within our breasts for regiment,
Doth teach us all to have aspiring minds:
Our souls, whose faculties can comprehend
The wondrous architecture of the world,
And measure every wand'ring planet's course,
Still climbing after knowledge infinite,
And always moving as the restless spheres,
Wills us to wear ourselves and never rest,
Until we reach the ripest fruit of all,
That perfect bliss and sole felicity,
The sweet fruition of an earthly crown.

This is his article of faith, the swelling prologue to the
imperial theme. The motive-force of life is, therefore,

[1] Roy Battenhouse, *Marlowe's Tamburlaine*, pp. 217–225.

the will to power unrestrained by morality. Marlowe had many such examples to draw upon in the Renaissance world, particularly the *condottiere* of Italy—'the terrible *male* italian tiger.'[1] If Tamburlaine starts as a shepherd, so did Carmagnola; Muzio Sforza began as a labourer, Nicolo Piccinini as a butcher. Moreover, Nature herself teaches us to have aspiring minds, for the very elements composing man's body are at war, and the soul itself is pure energy ranging the heavens for the knowledge and the comprehension which are another kind of power.

The height of Tamburlaine's ambition is, at first, the crown of Persia. 'A god,' he tells us, 'is not so glorious as a king.' The brief and pathetic encounter of the decadent Mycetes and the future world-conqueror betrays in Marlowe a rather surprising sympathy with weakness. There is in these scenes a certain tenderness, developed afterwards in his attitude to Edward II, but not elsewhere apparent in 'the stately tent of war', with the clash of arms, the marching and counter-marching of armies and the Miltonic roll of high-sounding names which accompanies the 'rogue of Asia's' rise to overlordship of the east. The imagery in which the Tartar's infinite ambition is bodied forth has a persistent quality of latent metaphysical thought which lifts what would otherwise have been rather a crude military pageant on to a plane of transcendent beauty. It must be confessed, however, that to a modern ear the uninterrupted flow of this high-pitched and loud-mouthed poetry becomes an intolerable ordeal. Even in its own time, the 'great and thundering speech' of Edward Alleyn, as he 'bestrid' the stage of the Rose in his coat of copper lace and his crimson velvet breeches,

[1] Wyndham Lewis, *The Lion and the Fox*, p. 59.

must have outroared the bulls of the adjacent bull ring. But the Elizabethans had stronger ears and stronger stomachs than ours.

As a justification of his conquests and the utter ruthlessness with which they are pursued, Tamburlaine, drawing upon a familiar Renaissance conception, tells us that he is the appointed Scourge of God and is therefore obliged to fulfil this terrible function. Having overcome his most powerful enemy, the Great Turk, he makes him his footstool and, mounting to his throne on Bajazeth's back, deliriously proclaims:

> Now clear the triple region of the air,
> And let the majesty of heaven behold
> Their Scourge and Terror tread on emperors.
> Smile stars that reign'd at my nativity:
> And dim the brightness of their neighbour lamps,
> Disdain to borrow light of Cynthia,
> For I the chiefest lamp of all the earth,
> First rising in the east with mild aspect,
> But fixed now in the meridian line,
> Will send up fire to your turning spheres,
> And cause the sun to borrow light of you.

As the stars were thought to take their light from the moon, he would, in his presumption, reverse the order of nature and cause his constellation not only to outshine the rest, but to give light to the sun itself. Tamburlaine has also more precise visions of world conquest, planning an empire that shall stretch 'Even from Persepolis to Mexico.'

In the siege of Damascus, Marlowe, following the later European historians, attributes to Tamburlaine the practice of ominously changing the colour of his tents from day to day. On the first day of the siege

Edward Alleyn

The Collier Leaf. Thought to be the first draft, in Marlowe's handwriting, of the scene of Mugeron's murder in The Massacre at Paris, beginning: "Enter a souldier with a muskett. Now sir, to you that dares make a duke a cuckolde and use a counter-feyt key to his privie chamber..."

Part of the letter from Thomas Kyd to Sir John Puckering, accusing Marlowe of atheism, beginning: "My first acquaintance with this Marlowe, rose upon his bearing name to serve my Lo: although his white tents indicate to the besieged that if they surrender-their lives will be spared; on the second day his red tents threaten that only those who are armed will be slain when he storms the town; on the third day, his black tents mean that all will be put to death, 'without respect of sex, degree or age.' In scene four of act four he 'comes in all in scarlet' and gives the command 'Now hang our bloody colours by Damascus.' He then sits down to banquet with Zenocrate and his generals before the city walls, and Bajazeth is brought in in his cage to provide entertainment. Tamburlaine advises the starving Turk to eat his wife before she gets too thin. This passage, so popular with the Elizabethan audience, is written in prose and it is usual to think that Marlowe was not responsible for its barbarous humour.

The next scene contains the famous massacre of the virgins of Damascus, who come to plead for their city. They come too late. Tamburlaine has already displayed his black colours and himself changed into funereal armour. 'What, are the the turtles frayed out of their nests?' he exclaims, 'Alas, poor fools . . .' He is sorry for them, but it is against his honour to deviate from his accustomed course, so they must die. After their 'slaughtered carcasses' have been hoisted on to the walls of Damascus, Tamburlaine shows that he is deeply moved by Zenocrate's anxiety for her father and the fate of Egypt. In her tear-filled eyes, he says,

> . . . angels in their crystal armours fight
> A doubtful battle with my tempted thoughts,
> For Egypt's freedom and the Soldan's life:
> His life that so consumes Zenocrate,
> Whose sorrows lay more siege unto my soul,
> Than all my army to Damascus' walls.

This is followed by the well-known passage on the inability of poets to express ultimate loveliness—reflections which may seem strange in a man who has just ordered the slaughter of a whole city population. But Tamburlaine is a more complicated character than at first appears and this is a crisis in his development. Zenocrate has flooded his mind with rapture, for she is beauty incarnate, and through her he feels pity for the first time. It is a puzzling and unwelcome experience. 'What is beauty saith my sufferings then?' he cries. An intricate speech shows the conflict in his mind. Out of love for Zenocrate he has promised to spare the Soldan's life and he fears lest this emotion of pity, inspired by beauty, shall make him effeminate. There is such a thing as being too merciful and this does not accord with his 'honour, which consists in shedding blood.' But beauty also inspires him with deeds of valour. Therefore he will both 'conceive' beauty and 'subdue' it, for 'Virtue solely is the sum of glory'— that is Roman *virtus*, vigour unimpaired.[1]

From these airy speculations it is a sharp descent to 'Hath Bajazeth been fed to-day?' but a descent necessary, perhaps, to recapture the wandering attention of the audience—and there follows the scene in which Bajazeth and his wife dash their brains out on the bars of their cage, a spectacle upon which Zenocrate moralizes, warning her love against placing his chiefest good in worldly pomp and putting his trust in 'slippery crowns.'

Tamburlaine Part I ends with gestures of magnanimity on the part of the conqueror, and it is clear that the influence of Zenocrate has brought about a certain reformation of his manners. He promises to give both

[1] G. I. Duthie, 'The Dramatic Structure of Marlowe's Tamburlaine the Great Parts I and II,' *English Studies*, 1948.

Bajazeth and Zabina honourable burial and to marry
Zenocrate, whose betrothed, the unfortunate King
of Arabia, has killed himself in chagrin. Turning to
his followers, Tamburlaine tells them to exchange
their armour for scarlet robes and make laws to rule
their several provinces—'For Tamburlaine takes truce
with all the world.'

When he came to write the second part of *Tamburlaine*,
in response to popular demand, Marlowe had already
exhausted his sources for the career of his hero. He
fell back, therefore, on a manipulation of Turkish
history, as found in Lonicerus's chronicle, combined
with a careful perusal of Ortelius's great atlas, the
Theatrum Orbis Terrarum. The Ortelius, as Mr. Bakeless
has shown, was in the library at Corpus Christi, and
how carefully Marlowe studied it can be seen from
his frequent location of different areas by their position
in relation to the tropic circles, and from the account
of Techelles' triumphal march through Africa, which
is simply a transcription of Ortelius's chief place-names,
together with his Latin notes.[1] Marlowe, in general,
followed his sources closely, but he does not mention
Tamburlaine's lameness. Tamburlaine, however, was
that same Timur the Lame (hence Timerlane) whom
the Spaniard Ruy Gonzalez de Clavijo visited as the
ambassador of Henry III of Castille and Leon in the year
1403.

At that time all Europe stood in awe of the almost
legendary conquests of Timur, who had carried his
Asiatic dominion to the very gates of Christendom.
Henry III was not alone in sending his congratulations
to the conqueror. Charles VI of France and Henry IV

---

[1] *Christopher Marlowe*, p. 62; and Ethel Seaton, 'Marlowe's Map,' *Essays and Studies* (vol. x), 1924.

of England had already anticipated him. Clavigo's account of his embassy to Samarcand was printed in Seville in 1582 and when he comes to describe the beauty and magnificence of all he saw, words fail him. He gives the following description of Timur. 'Timur Beg was seated in a portal, in front of the entrance to a beautiful palace; he was sitting on the ground. Before him there was a fountain, which threw up the water very high, and in it there were some red apples. The lord was seated cross-legged amongst round pillows on a silken embroidered carpet. He was dressed in a robe of plain silk without any embroidery, with a high white hat on his head, on the top of which there was a spinel ruby, with pearls and precious stones round it.' On meeting Clavijo, Timur enquired courteously after the health of 'his son' the King of Spain, who, he said, 'is the greatest king of the Franks, and lives at the end of the world.' A feast followed, and roasted and boiled sheep and horses were brought in on great leather plates. 'When the lord called for meat, the people dragged it to him on these leather dishes, so great was its weight; and as soon as it was within twenty paces of him, the carvers came, who cut it up, kneeling on the ground . . . so much of this food was brought that it was quite wonderful.' Clavijo describes another feast at which Timur sat in state in a central pavilion, on a divan in front of a silver-gilt screen, the walls hung with rose-coloured silk and ornamented with silver spangles, emeralds, pearls and tassels, which waved in the breeze after a fashion very pleasant to see. A slight *fracas* occurred, however, when the Spanish ambassadors, having waited for the interpreter, arrived late for the feast. This put Timur into a great rage. 'He sent for the interpreter and said, "How is it that you have caused me to be enraged and put out? Why were you not with the Frank ambassadors? I order that a hole be bored through your nose, that a cord be passed through it, and that you be led through the camp, as a warning to all.''' But one of Timur's councillors interceded for the unfortunate interpreter and the general good humour was restored.

For a feast a week later, Timur moved to another garden and the guests were told that they might drink wine, which they were not allowed to do otherwise, even in private. So much wine was drunk on this occasion, says Clavijo, that the whole court got completely drunk and everybody began to roll about on the ground. 'This was very jovial,' he adds, 'for they think there is no pleasure without drunken men.' At the height of the feasting, Timur ordered a gallows to be set up, declaring that he knew how to be merciful and kind to some, and how to be severe to others. The first victim was Dina, the chief magistrate of Samarcand, who, during Timur's absence, had used his office to misgovern the city. He was forthwith taken and hanged. A friend of Dina's, who interceded for him, was likewise hanged. The request of a courtier to buy Dina's pardon with four hundred thousand pesantes was first granted. He was then tortured for more money and, having none, hanged by his feet till he died. Several butchers were then beheaded for selling meat above the regulation price. After these pieces of justice, Timur's favourite wife appeared. Fifteen women carried her train, and she wore a crested head-dress of red cloth with white plumes. Her hair was black and hung round her shoulders. She was preceded by a guard of eunuchs and followed by three hundred women, and as she sat down, slightly behind her husband, three women steadied her head-dress so that it should not fall off. Then eight other wives, dressed in the same manner, came out of the pavilion and grouped themselves round Timur in the order of their rank in his affections. In front of this extraordinary group, jugglers, elephants and acrobats on trapezes performed.[1]

Timur had a passion for architecture—largely, it is to be feared, from motives of self-glorification—and his lifelong dream was to make Samarcand the most beautiful city in the world. To Samarcand he brought the scholars and filigree workers of Baghdad, the Ming artists of China, the white marble of Tabriz, the glazed tiles of Herat, and the clear jade of Khotan. He set up libraries, academies of philosophy and science, observatories, menageries and aviaries. Upon his Palace of Heart's Delight, a dazzling vision of marble, porcelain and turquoise, set in groves of blossoming fruit trees and terraced gardens with their clear streams and fountains amidst beds of tulips, he lavished the skill of Persian gardeners, Chinese, Indian and Persian painters. In directing his building operations, Timur was autocratic in the extreme. No sooner had a mosque been built than, we are told, he was sure to find something wrong with it and would order it to be pulled down and rebuilt in ten days. If it was not finished in that time, the builders paid for it with their lives. These feverish building operations have frequently been represented by the Timurid School of Persian painters. It was Timur's ambition to restore the empire of Ghengis Khan. In this he failed, but by comparison with him Ghengis was a rude barbarian. One Persian source tells us that Timur reverenced learning and that

[1] *Narrative of the Embassy of Ruy Gonzalez de Clavigo to the Court of Timour of Samarkand, A.D. 1403–6.* Translated by Clements B. Markham.

when he took a city he spared scholars, artists, mosques and hospitals. Marlowe, apparently, knew none of this, but he was near the truth when he gave Tamburlaine his own sadism and radiant sense of beauty.

Tamburlaine Part II remains in form the same kind of extended military pageant as Part I. But images of darkness, as presages of downfall, begin to encroach upon the ethereal glow of the verse. Consumed by his choleric humour, an increasing frenzy drives this rival of the gods into delusion and madness, and Marlowe begins to see his hero in a light that is dangerously near to burlesque.

Tamburlaine now has three sons by Zenocrate, but their mild and beautiful aspect disappoints him. Their hair, he complains, is white as milk and soft as down, when it should be 'like the quills of porpentines, as black as jet, and hard as iron or steel.' Worse still, Calyphas, his 'coward' son, objects that surely his father has won enough territory already. His brothers, he says, can go on conquering the world, if they are so minded. As for himself, he prefers to stay with his mother. Such unheroic sentiments produce the expected explosion of rage from the Scourge of God, who tells Calyphas that he who means to occupy his throne after his death 'Must armèd wade up to the chin in blood.' Zenocrate, with her usual softening and moderating influence, objects that such a picture might discourage her other two sons from a military career. By no means, says one of them, if his father's throne were floating in a sea of blood, he would sail to it in a ship. The other adds that, as for him, he would either swim through blood to his father's throne, or make a bridge of carcasses, whose arches should be framed with the bones of Turks. 'Well, lovely boys,' says Tamburlaine, 'you shall be emperors both.'

Throughout both parts of *Tamburlaine* Marlowe is constantly turning over in his mind various forms of religious belief, only to find them wanting, if not actually absurd. His own belief appears to have been in a divine principle of energy, which

> Nor in one place is circumscriptible,
> But everywhere fills every continent
> With strange infusion of his sacred vigour

This subtle conception, however, appears to be continually at war in the poet's mind with the more conventional idea of a god sitting in heaven and periodically chastising his naughty children like an angry father, and it is against this conception that Marlowe is in rebellion. Tamburlaine is, not unnaturally, chiefly interested in the military prowess of the Diety, whereever or whatever he might be. Obviously he believed in a god of some sort, otherwise there would be no point in calling himself the Scourge of God. Nevertheless, as the second part of *Tamburlaine* proceeds, he becomes increasingly sceptical about the power, or even the existence, of such a god, and his attitude to him is one of growing insolence.

The great crisis in the second part is the death of Zenocrate. It is his first defeat at the hands of a power he cannot control and proof that Death is not his servant, as he had come to believe. In spite of his claim to be the equal of the gods, Tamburlaine now discovers that though he can take life, he cannot give it or prolong it. This discovery makes all his conquests vain; for he is struck by the thought that he may even be mortal himself. As the curtains at the back of the stage are drawn aside to reveal the dying Zenocrate

on her bed of state, Tamburlaine's imagination once
more takes wing upon one of its unparalleled lyrical
flights. As the verse rises and mounts and wheels into
the sky, it takes on the strophic form of an ode. When
Zenocrate dies, Tamburlaine's fury knows no bounds.

What, is she dead? Techelles, draw thy sword,
And wound the earth, that it may cleave in twain,
And we descend into th'infernal vaults,
To hale the fatal sisters by the hair,
And throw them in the triple moat of hell. . . .
Raise cavalieros higher than the clouds,
And with the cannon break the frame of heaven,
Better the shining palace of the sun,
And shiver all the starry firmament:

Since all this is impossible, he contents himself by
burning down Larissa, where Zenocrate died—'the
houses burnt will look as if they mourn'd.'

Tamburlaine's lecture to his sons on the fortification
and besieging of a town is borrowed from Paul Ive's
Practise of Fortification, and the description of the siege
of Balsera closely follows the technique of sixteenth-
century warfare, with which Marlowe appears to be
quite familiar.[1] Calyphas, however, objects that it all
sounds rather dangerous, whereupon, after the usual
explosion of fury, Tamburlaine asks:

Hast thou beheld a peal of ordnance strike
A ring of pikes, mingled with shot and horse,
Whose shattered limbs, being tossed as high as
heaven,
Hang in the air as thick as sunny motes,
And canst thou, coward, stand in fear of death?

[1] Paul Ive was both a Kentishman and a diplomatic courier, and thus possibly
a friend of Marlowe's. He dedicated his *Practise of Fortification* to Sir Francis
Walsingham. As this work was not published until 1589, Marlowe must
have read it in manuscript.

H

Such a delectable sight is, from Tamburlaine's point of view, though not necessarily from Marlowe's, sufficient to banish any initial distaste for warfare. But Marlowe continues to give Calyphas sceptical and satirical lines which increasingly tend to deflate the image of his father. Tamburlaine lances his own arm to demonstate how trivial a thing is a wound and invites his other sons to wash in his blood. Thus they partake of the ancient blood covenant of many primitive religions, which, in its Mithraic form, was popular in the Roman army.

Tamburlaine's action in stabbing Calyphas for cowardice and so silencing the one remaining voice of reason in the play—though such an action would probably be regarded by an Elizabethan audience as an example of heroic martial justice—is accompanied by an increasing megalomania. He threatens Jove with greater enmity, for giving him such a son, 'than he that darted mountains at thy head.'

From the time when Tamburlaine enters in act four in his coach drawn by the conquered kings, he is little more than a madman. Standing up in his outrageous coach, he addresses his human horses with the 'Holla, ye pampered jades of Asia' speech which became, with Kyd's 'O eyes, no eyes, but fountains fraught with tears,' the most famous lines in Elizabethan drama.

The lines continue to mount in a blazing crescendo while Tamburlaine plans the rebuilding of Samarcand. He sees himself riding like Jupiter in triumph through the streets, in a chariot gilt with fire, as emperor of the threefold world, while all the gods stand gazing at his pomp. After the capture of Babylon, the governor is hung up in chains on the walls and shot to death,

the citizens are bound hand and foot and thrown into
the lake, together with their wives and children.
'Drown them all,' shouts Tamburlaine, 'man, woman
and child, leave not a Babylonian in the town.' His
human horses, having grown broken-winded, are also
hanged and two 'spare' kings are harnessed in their
place. Tamburlaine's triumph is now complete. He
dares Mahomet to come down from heaven and avenge
the slaughter of the faithful, and he burns the Koran.
Soon after this final blasphemy he begins to sicken and,
concluding that his sickness has been sent by some god
to torment him, prepares to levy war against heaven.

> Come let us march against the powers of heaven,
> And set black streamers in the firmament,
> To signify the slaughter of the gods.

In his delirium, he tells Techelles to go up to the court
of Jove and command him to send Apollo down to
cure his sickness, 'or I'll fetch him down myself.'
But the doctor's verdict is ominous. The doctor tells
him that his urine is thick and this makes his danger
great. Moreover, his veins are 'full of accidental heat,
Whereby the moisture of your blood is dried.' Worse,
the *humidum* and *calor*, which some hold to be 'of a
substance more divine and pure,' is almost extinguished
and spent. In short, Tamburlaine has paid the penalty
of his choleric humour. Calling for a map of the world,
he surveys it to see how much land is left unconquered
so that his sons may carry on the good work after his
death. As in his rhapsody in praise of the dying Zenocrate Tamburlaine's imperial dreams now fall naturally
into the strophes of an ode, with the refrain 'And
shall I die and this unconquered?' Like Ralegh, he
enchants us with visions of undiscovered worlds,

regretting that he now no longer has time to cut his projected channel from Alexandria to the Red Sea ('That men might quickly sail to India') and that the riches of so many new lands must remain unexploited:

> Whereas the sun declining from our sight,
> Begins the day with our antipodes.

When he dies, we are told that his flesh is 'not of force enough to hold the fiery spirit it contains,' and that heaven has 'consumed his choicest living fire.'

(iii) THE JEW OF MALTA

Written c. 1591

Published. Entered in the Stationer's Register on 17 May 1594 to Nicholas Ling and Thomas Millington as *The Famous Tragedy of the Rich Jew of Malta*. The earliest extant edition is that of 1633.

Stage history. Performed by Lord Strange's men on 26 February 1592, but not as a new play. 'The Jew' was one of the most popular plays in Henslowe's repertory, thirty-six performances being recorded in his famous diary up 21 June 1596. It was revived in 1601 at Henslowe's theatre and again in 1633, first at Court and then at the Cockpit in Drury Lane, under the supervision of Thomas Heywood.

Sources. Possibly Philip Lonicerus's *Chronicorum Turcicorum* and Belleforest's *Cosmographie Universelle*, where the career of the Portuguese Jew Juan Miques bears some resemblance to Barabas's. Professor Tucker Brooke thinks it more likely, however, that David Passi, a Jew of Constantinople, involved in the Turkish designs against Malta, playing off Turk against Christian, was the original of Barabas. Passi was also connected with English diplomacy in the Mediterranean and his career came to an end in 1591. Marlowe may have known of his activities at first hand through his contact with the secret service. Several families of wealthy and influential Jews were resident in Elizabethan London at his time. Among them was the famous Alvaro Mendez, a kinsman of Miques. A fierce quarrel, well-known in diplomatic circles, developed between these two men during 1591-2. See H. S. Bennett's edition, pp. 11-12.

Plot. The Prologue introduces the ghost of Machiavelli, who informs the audience that he has come from France 'to frolic with his friends' and 'to present the tragedy of a Jew.' He retires and Barabas is shown gloating over 'infinite riches in a little room,' where he is visited shortly by the other Jewish merchants of Malta. They tell him that by a new decree of the Senate, every Jew of Malta must either surrender half his estate to the Treasury, or become a Christian, for the Governor of the island has decided to collect the Turkish tribute from the Jewish community, on the plea that Malta has brought a curse upon itself by harbouring Jews. All the Jews except Barabas agree to part with half their estates. Barabas stoutly refuses to give up either his money or his religion. Whereupon the Maltese knights confiscate what they believe to be his entire fortune and convert his house into a nunnery. Barabas, who is 'fram'd of finer mould than common men,' has already made provision for any possible loss or calamity. He tells his daughter, Abigail, to seek admission to the nunnery, on the plea that she wants to make atonement for her lack of faith. There, hidden beneath the floor, she will find the rest of their wealth, which amounts to as much as the State had already confiscated.

Barabas now lives only for revenge. He strikes at Farnese, the Governor, through his son, Lodowick, who visits him in the hope of catching a glimpse of his beautiful daughter. Barabas persuades Abigail to feign love for Lodowick, though she is really in love with Don Mathias, Lodowick's best friend, and has left the nunnery on his account. Barabas forges a challenge from Lodowick to Don Mathias: they fight and kill each other. Appalled at such villainy, Abigail returns to the nunnery. Her father, fearing that she will give him away during confession, presents her with a pot of poisoned porridge, which also poisons the entire convent. But Abigail has already confessed and two friars of rival orders now visit the Jew to denounce him. A farcical scene follows in which Barabas pretends that he wants to be converted to Christianity and the friars come to blows in their zeal to have the credit of converting him and laying hands on his wealth. With the aid of his Turkish slave, Ithamore, Barabas strangles one of the friars and disposes of the other by accusing him of murder. Ithamore now begins to blackmail him, for the sake of the courtesan Bellamira, and Barabas gets rid of both of them by the gift of a bunch of poisoned flowers. Before they die, they reveal all his crimes to the Governor. Barabas is condemned to death, but escapes execution by drugging himself and is given up for dead. On the return of the Turks to besiege Malta in default of the tribute money, he betrays the city to them and is made Governor in place of Farnese, who is delivered to him by Calymath. Instead of putting Farnese to death, Barabas strikes a bargain with him to deliver Calymath and the whole Turkish force into his hands. His plans miscarry and he falls into the cauldron of boiling water he had prepared for Calymath.

The Jew of Malta, with Kyd's *The Spanish Tragedy*, was one of the two plays which gave birth to the type of the Machiavellian villain on the English stage. In the Prologue, Machiavelli announces:

Admir'd I am of those that hate me most.
Though some speak openly against my books,
Yet will they read me. . . .
I count religion but a childish toy,
And hold there is no sin but ignorance.
Birds of the air will tell of murders past?
I am asham'd to hear such fooleries.
Many will talk of title to a crown.
What right had Caesar to the empery?

Might first made kings, and laws were then most sure
When like the Draco's they were writ in blood.
Hence comes it, that a strong built citadel
Commands much more than letters can import.

As a matter of fact, the real Machiavelli believed
just the opposite: it was Gentillet, in his popular work
Contre N. Machiavel, who credited him with these
views. Marlowe had probably read Machiavelli at
Cambridge and, as we have seen, there is some reason
for believing that his friend Kyd transcribed for the
press the only Elizabethan translation of *The Prince*.
But in *The Jew of Malta* it is Gentillet he draws upon,
rather than the Florentine, for his picture of a pure
'Machiavellian' villain. Machiavelli attached far too great
an importance to religion, as an instrument of policy,
ever to regard it as 'a childish toy.' As for fortresses,
he had very little use for them. In both *The Prince* and
the *Discorsi* he says explicitly that they do more harm
than good. He also deprecated avoidable cruelty in a
prince. But Gentillet had written that the evil influence
of Machiavelli was embodied in the duke of Guise
and Catherine de Medicis, while the Bartholomew
massacre was shown as a typically Machiavellian event.
Needless to say, Machiavelli's teaching, which initiated
a new era in political thinking, was far more subtle
than it is represented to be either by Gentillet or in
this play.[1]

There could scarcely be a greater contrast to the
heroic rapture of *Tamburlaine* than this savage comedy.
After the first act, where Barabas appears as a great Jewish
merchant dominating everyone around him by the force

[1] A similar caricature of Machiavelli's thought is given by Gabriel Harvey
in a Latin epigram published in *Gratulationum Valdinenses Libri Quattuor* (1578),
where Machiavelli speaks in person, as in the prologue to *The Jew of Malta*.

of his intelligence and by his almost mystical devotion to gold, he dwindles into a skinny figure of hatred; motivated solely by cunning, cruelty and lust, the proud aspiring verse degenerates into an electric crackle of irony and malice. Having shown us Renaissance man as he would be in the figure of Tamburlaine, here Marlowe shows us Renaissance men and women as they really were.

The action is worked out with the calculated coldness of a game of chess. Most of the game Barabas is one move ahead of the Christians and, though he skilfully plays one character off against another, like a clever politician, he is checkmated in the end. Like Tamburlaine, Barabas also has his infinite ambition. This time, as we are now in the world of men, it is power through money that he covets and commands.

> Who hateth me but for my happiness?
> Or who is honoured now but for his wealth?
> Rather had I a Jew be hated thus,
> Than pitied in a Christian poverty:
> For I can see no fruits in all their faith,
> But malice, falsehood and excessive pride,
> Which methinks fits not their profession.
> Haply some hapless man hath conscience,
> And for his conscience lives in beggary.

This view of things is only too well borne out in the great scene with Farnese and the Maltese knights, who, after taking all the Jew's goods, tell him that if he is ruined thereby that is not their fault but his inherent sin. 'What?' exclaims Barabas, genuinely outraged,

> What? bring you Scripture to confirm your wrongs?
> Preach me not out of my possessions!

to which Farnese replies, with self-conscious virtue:

> Excess of wealth is cause of covetousness:
> And covetousness, O 'tis a monstrous sin!

Barabas asks him bitterly, now that he has ruined him, whether Farnese would like to take his life as well. Farnese replies in the very words with which the Church justified the burning of heretics:

> No, Barabas, to stain our hands with blood
> Is far from us and our profession.

Better one man want for the common good, he tells him, than many perish for a private man, where the reference is to the decision of the chief priests and Pharisees to deliver Jesus over to execution—a reference not immediately apparent in this context, but to Marlowe doubtless a source of malicious humour.

Much of the comedy of *The Jew of Malta* is of this acid, subliminal kind and is reinforced by Marlowe's use of the aside as a sort of private joke. While Barabas gets the better of the argument morally, Marlowe by no means intends to hold up Judaism as an alternative to Christianity. His aim is to show that it is, at any rate, just as good—or, rather, just as bad. Farnese breaks his promise to the Turks, on the ground that he is not bound to keep faith with infidels; Barabas justifies his deception of both Christians and Turks, since in his view all are heretics that are not Jews. The only people who behave honourably are the Turks.

Marlowe is quite safe indulging in this rather dangerous by-play, because his audience would see the villainy of the Jew to the exclusion of all else and so miss the more subtle thrusts. After the first act, Barabas's villainy is laid on so thick that he becomes not much more than a paste-board figure of melodrama—and melodrama that is very near to burlesque. The rest of the play, devoted as it is to the Jew's revenge, is not tragedy to a modern view, for the motives of all concerned are so mean that we do not care what becomes of any of them, and it is with a feeling near to relief that we watch Barabas fall into his cauldron at last. Still less is it a comedy, in the accepted sense, though there is no mistaking the ironical flippancy with which Marlowe surrounds the most atrocious deeds. The dominant feeling aroused by *The Jew of Malta* is nearer to that provoked by a Punch and Judy show—but a Punch and Judy show on a horrifying scale.

Nowhere does Barabas become a great tragic figure like Shylock, and nowhere is the difference between Marlowe and Shakespeare so apparent as in their handling of anti-semitism. Marlowe exaggerates it until it becomes a farce; Shakespeare reveals Shylock's humanity even when he is spitting venom. Barabas is pure cold-blooded venom.

> In spite of these swine-eating Christians
> (Unchosen nation, never circumcis'd,
> Such as, poor villains, were ne'er thought upon
> Till Titus and Vespasian conquer'd us,)
> Am I become as wealthy as I was . . .
> I am not of the tribe of Levy, I,
> That can so soon forget an injury.
> We Jews can fawn like spaniels when we please;
> And when we grin we bite. . . .

But apart from the figure of Shylock, *The Merchant of Venice* has none of the wit and headlong, furious energy of *The Jew of Malta*. With its colourless merchant and silly business of the caskets, it is, in fact, rather a foolish comedy—apart from the fine court scene and the lovely moonlight scene at the end—and would doubtless have been called *The Jew of Venice* had it not been preceded by Marlowe's play.[1]

Before the terrifying and horrible scene between Barabas and the 'two religious caterpillars', Barabas councels his slave and accomplice Ithamore:

> First be thou void of these affections:
> Compassion, love, vain hope, and heartless fear;
> Be mov'd at nothing, see thou pity none. . . .

When Friar Jacomo returns to Barabas's house in the hope of converting him to Christianity and, incidentally, getting hold of his money, he finds his way barred at the door by the figure of Friar Barnardine. But Barnardine is already dead, having just been strangled on the open stage with cords by Barabas and Ithamore, who have now propped the corpse up in the doorway on his staff, 'as if he were begging of bacon.' Thinking that Barnardine is trying to prevent him from entering the house, Jacomo strikes him down and Barabas and Ithamore promptly accuse him of murder. 'What?' cries Barabas, 'a friar a murderer? When shall you see a Jew commit the like?' The irony of this consists in the fact that Barabas would not waste his time striking dead men, and to Jacomo's pleadings to be allowed to escape he replies with grim relish:

> No, pardon me, the law must have its course.
> Take in the staff too, for that must be shown.
> Law wills that each particular be known.

In the scenes where Ithamore, Bellamira and Pilia-Borza discuss the best ways of extorting money from Barabas, Marlowe ridicules some of the more absurd prejudices against Jews, just as earlier Jacomo had

---

[1] It was, in fact, entered as such in the Stationers' Register.

eagerly asked Barnardine: 'What, has he crucified a child?' Ithamore tells them that his master lives on pickled grasshoppers, that he never changes his shirt, that the hat he wears was left by Judas under the elm tree when he hanged himself.

When at last the law catches up with Barabas, Farnese, true to the methods of interrogation of those days, cries: 'Make fires, heat irons, let the rack be fetch'd.' And he has to be reminded by one of the knights that perhaps Barabas will confess without such persuasion. Barabas, however, acts to the last according to his Machiavellian principles. After the Turks have installed him as Governor of Malta, he only thinks of how much money he can wring out of Farnese by betraying Calymath.

> Thus loving neither, will I live with both,
> Making a profit of my policy;
> And he from whom my most advantage comes,
> Shall be my friend.
> This is the life we Jews are us'd to lead;
> And reason too, for Christians do the like.

It is excellent policy, but this time Barabas has double-crossed once too often and it is Farnese who cuts the cable while the Jew is standing in the gallery welcoming his Turkish guests. He falls into his own trap and dies, scalded to death, cursing the 'damn'd Christians, dogs, and Turkish infidels.' Farnese, nevertheless, benefits by the Jew's stratagem, keeping Calymath prisoner until he has made peace on his own terms, the main Turkish force having been meanwhile blown up in a monastery according to plan. The play concludes with lines that provide the last ironical twist of the knife:

> So march away, and let due praise be given
> Neither to Fate nor Fortune, but to Heaven.

It was T. S. Eliot who first suggested that *The Jew of Malta* should be regarded as a farce—'farce of the old English humour, the terribly serious, even savage comic humour . . . of that very serious (but very different) play *Volpone*.' Marlowe, he thinks, conceived Barabas as 'a prodigious caricature.' But H. S. Bennett, the latest editor of the play, objects: 'This view seems to postulate considerable powers of detachment from contemporary taste and practice on the part of Marlowe.' We should, he thinks, see the play as a tragedy of blood in the manner of *The Spanish Tragedy*. Certainly there is nothing farcical about the first act. It was Marlowe's mistake to conceive Barabas on too grand a scale to begin with and then to allow himself to be carried away by a mood of burlesque in the remaining acts. Apparently he was unable to sustain his original conception when the plot began to move.

Marlowe's genius is peculiar for the split it shows between lyrical ardour and the critical faculty. This gave rise not only to mockery of others, but to the self-mockery of the frustrated idealist. Thus we find the villainous Ithamore serenading the whore Bellamira with a cynical parody of his author's most famous lyric, 'Come live with me and be my love.'

(iv) THE MASSACRE AT PARIS

Written 1591–2.

Published. Printed by Edward Allde for Edward White, 'dwelling near the little north door of S. Paules Church, at the sign of the Gun.' This octavo is undated and probably based on a stolen prompt book.

Stage history. First acted by Strange's men at the Rose as 'The Tragedy of the Guise' in January 1593 and marked by

Henslowe as a new play. The takings at this performance were £3. 14s.—the highest of the season, the average takings for other plays being £1 14s. Staged again by the Admiral's men at the Rose on 19 June 1594. On 18 January 1602 Admiral's bought it from Edward Alleyn, with two other plays, for £6.

Sources. Jean de Serres's *Commentaries of the Civill Warres in Fraunce* Book X, translated by T. Timme in 1576; also possibly de Serres's *The Life of Jasper Coligny* (1576).

Plot. The play opens with the marriage of King Charles IX's sister Margaret to Henry of Navarre. This enrages the Duke of Guise, since it unites Catholics ånd Huguenots. Guise orders an apothecary to present a pair of poisoned gloves to the Queen Mother of Navarre, who has contrived the match. Admiral Coligny is then shot through the arm by a soldier from an upper window. These crimes are the prelude to the Massacre of St. Bartholomew, in which Guise has for his chief confederates the Queen Mother, Catherine de Medicis, and the Duke of Anjou. The king, Charles IX, is irresolute but allows himself to be overruled. He visits the Lord Admiral and assures him of royal protection, then signs the order for the Bartholomew massacre, which begins with the murder of the Admiral in his bed. Catherine de Medicis poisons Charles IX, her son, and Henry III comes to the throne. Henry gives himself up to a life of pleasure and Catherine and Guise plan to rule France through him. He over-reaches them in 'policy' and has Guise and the Cardinal of Lorraine assassinated, only to be stabbed by a Jacobin friar. As he dies he calls for the English ambassador and tells him to relate all he has seen to his mistress, Queen Elizabeth, and urges Navarre to avenge his death on the Catholics.

The play has come down to us in a text so fragmentary and corrupt as to suggest that what we have is no more than a version based on a theatrical prompt book.

Nevertheless, this probably represents the substance of the drama as Marlowe conceived it. It has many parallels with the second and third parts of *Henry VI* and with *Edward II*, which, without taking into consideration the question of their priority or otherwise, indicates that all these plays were written about the same time— that is, in the years 1591-2. In the first half of *The Massacre*, Marlowe follows de Serres closely, but no single source can be traced for the scenes which follow the accession of Henry III, and here, it is thought, Marlowe relied on contemporary gossip and rumour. As a secret agent, or with friends in the secret service, he was in a better position to hear the 'inside story' than most other Elizabethan playwrights. The atrocious subject matter seems, as usual, to have inspired him with a certain exhilaration, and the play appears to have been written at breathless speed. It dealt with events that were still in the news and, doubtless, provided a useful testimony to its author's patriotic Protestantism and loyalty at a time when they were being rather more than questioned among his friends.

As we have seen from The Prologue to *The Jew of Malta*, the duke of Guise was popularly regarded as the reincarnation of Machiavelli this side of the Alps and the Bartholomew massacre was thought to be directly inspired by Machiavelli, to the extent that *The Prince* was known as 'the bible of the Queen Mother,' Catherine de Medicis. In his ruthlessness and craft, Guise is akin to Barabas, in the infinite scope of his ambition to Tamburlaine. He is even more arrogantly inhuman and brutally precise than either. As Marlowe conceives him, though the leader of the Catholic party in France, he uses religion merely as an instrument of policy:

Religion! *O Diabole!*
Fie, I am ashamed, however that I seem,
To think a word of such a simple sound
Of so great matter should be made the ground!

The real aim of the duke is the crown.

The play, which is not divided into either scenes or acts, proceeds from treachery to treachery and provides the audience with a murder every few minutes. As a loose chronicle play, it is written with great vigour and, in the soliloquies of Guise, contains passages of terrible and Satanic poetry. His first great speech sets the tone of the play:

> If ever Hymen lour'd at marriage rites,
> And had his altars deck'd with dusky lights:
> If ever sun stain'd heaven with bloody clouds,
> And made it look with terror on the world:
> If ever day were turn'd to ugly night,
> And night made semblance of the hue of hell,
> This day, this hour, this fatal night,
> Shall fully shew the fury of them all.

After telling his apothecary to present poisoned gloves to the Queen of Navarre, Guise lays bare his mind, in the manner of Richard III, in a remarkable speech of nearly two pages, elaborating Marlowe's creed of the Superman with its doctrine of dangerous living.

> Oft have I levell'd, and at last have learn'd,
> That peril is the chiefest way to happiness,
> And resolution honour's fairest aim.
> What glory is there in a common good,
> That hangs for every peasant to achieve?
> That like I best that flies beyond my reach . . .
> Although my downfall be the deepest hell.

Admiral Coligny is then murdered in his sick-bed and his body thrown out of the window into the street—that is, on the Elizabethan stage, from the upper chamber (or first balcony) down to the platform. A scene is devoted to the murder of Ramus—a strange academic interlude in the general orgy of slaughter. Ramus, in his *Dialectica*, had attacked the Aristotelian system and Guise explains to him why he must die.

> Was it not thou that scoff'dst the *Organon*,
> And said it was a heap of vanities?
> He that will be a flat dichotomist,
> And seen in nothing but epitomes,
> Is in your judgement thought a learned man;
> And he, forsooth, must go and preach in Germany . . .
> To contradict which, I say Ramus shall die.
> How answer you that? your *nego argumentum*
> Cannot serve, sirrah. Kill him.

We have only to substitute Marx for Aristotle to bring this passage up to date. The poor man's last-minute recantation cannot save him.

> I knew the *Organon* to be confus'd,
> And I reduc'd it into better form.
> And this for Aristotle will I say,
> That he that despiseth him can ne'er
> Be good in logic or philosophy.

But it's no good. The Guise only reiterates, 'Stab him, I say, and send him to his friends in hell!'

The tide of massacre engulfs the stage, and after the murder of the king, who has inconvenient scruples about killing so many of his subjects, Catherine de Medicis begins to assume the aspect of the Queen in *Alice in Wonderland*, with her 'Tush, all shall die unless

I have my will!'—her will being to rule France through her other son Henry III. 'His mind, you see,' she explains 'runs on his minions.'

An unpleasant little episode, which Marlowe introduced from a contemporary chapbook, occurs at the coronation of Henry III. Mugeroun, one of the king's 'minions,' loses a gold button off his cloak, and, turning suddenly, cuts off the ear of the man who has stolen it. 'Come, sir,' he says, 'give me my button and here's your ear.' The same cruel humour comes out again in the Cade and Simpcox scenes in *Henry VI*, which Marlowe may have written, for they are unlike anything else in Shakespeare.

But Henry III is not so enfeebled by his life of pleasure as not to be aware of the designs of the duke and his mother. He is presented as a typically Machiavellian figure, with a smile about as wholesome as a serpent's, who over-reaches the duke of Guise in guile. Guise has much of the overweening arrogance of Shakespeare's Julius Caesar. 'Guise, wear our crown,' Henry tells him ironically, 'and be thou king of France, And as dictator make or war or peace, Whilst I cry *placet* like a senator.' True to his imperial pretensions, Guise vows to make Henry follow his chariot wheels, 'as ancient Romans their captive lords.' At last, warned that assassins are lying in wait for him, he exclaims, like Shakespeare's Caesar:

> Yet Caesar shall go forth.
> Let mean conceits, and baser men fear death.
> Tut, they are peasants: *I* am Duke of Guise,
> And princes with their looks engender fear.

It has been argued by Robertson, on the strength of this passage and the similarity of some of the lines to

Marlowe's accepted work, that Marlowe was the original author of *Julius Caesar*. It is more likely that Shakespeare reverted, unconsciously perhaps, to this passage in a very popular play when he was writing *Julius Caesar* ten years later. Bakeless has pointed out that the Catholic party in France habitually referred to Guise as Caesar.

The general massacre now begins to turn in the other direction. When Henry sees the body of Guise, he cries in fiendish delight:

> Ah this sweet sight is physic to my soul,
> Go fetch his son for to behold his death.
> Surcharg'd with guilt of thousand massacres,
> Mounser of Lorraine sink away to hell. . . .
> This is the traitor that hath spent my gold
> In making foreign wars and civil broils.
> Did he not draw a sort of English priests
> From Douai to the seminary at Rheims,
> To hatch forth treason 'gainst their natural queen?[1]
> Did he not cause the King of Spain's huge fleet
> To threaten England and to menace me?

For all his heterodox speculation and blasphemous table talk, it is surprising how orthodox the conclusions of Marlowe's plays invariably are. In *The Massacre at Paris*, Machiavellism is shown as an evil philosophy in the service of the Counter-Reformation and the play concludes with a resounding patriotic Protestantism. With his dying breath, Henry calls for the English ambassador and sends loving messages to the Queen of England, 'whom God hath blessed for hating papistry,' and he bids the weeping Epernoun to dry his tears

[1] The college at Rheims was under the patronage of the duke of Guise.

and whet his sword on Sixtus' bones, 'That it may keenly slice the Catholics.'

The real characters in this drama were quite as unpleasant as Marlowe depicts them. On the walls of the Uffizi at Florence hangs a series of tapestries commemorating the fantastic extravagance of the French court at this period. The pale disagreeable faces of these Renaissance princes, accompanied by their minions and lords temporal and spiritual, look out at us down the centuries with the expressions of vultures, while in the background a soldier flings a ball of wildfire among the rearing horses at a military tournament, and warships discharge their cannon against Leviathan on an artificial lake.

(v) EDWARD THE SECOND

Written 1591–2.

Published. Entered in the Stationers' Register to William Jones on 6 July 1593, and printed by him in 1594 and sold at his shop near Holborn Conduit at the Sign of the Gun. Of this quarto, whose title page runs: The troublesome raigne and lamentable death of Edward the Second, King of England: with the tragicall fall of proud Mortimer . . . written by Chr: Marlowe *Gent*—two copies exist. One is in the Landesbibliothek of Cassel and the other in Zentralbibliothek at Zurich. An imperfect copy of an edition purporting to be that of 1593, with the first two leaves and seventy lines of the text in a seventeenth century hand, is in the South Kensington Museum, London.

Stage history. Published as 'sundry times publically acted in the honourable city of London by the right honourable the earl of Pembroke his servants.' Pembroke's acted at Court in December 1592 and January 1593, when they may have given *Edward II.* They would have acted it, probably at the Theatre, shortly after. Revived by Queen Anne's men at the Red Bull, Clerkenwell, between 1604 and 1617.

Sources. Principally Holinshed's *Chronicles* and Stow's *Annals.*

Plot. Piers Gaveston, the King's favourite, returns from banishment in spite of the barons' opposition. The King and Gaveston assault the Bishop of Coventry, after which outrage the Archbishop of Canterbury and the barons re-enact Gaveston's banishment in the Temple. Edward makes his favourite Governor of Ireland. At the instigation of Queen Isabella, who hopes in this way to recover her husband's affection, Gaveston is once more recalled. Gaveston insults the barons and accuses Isabella of unfaithfulness with the Younger Mortimer. The nobles then resort to arms to compel the king to give up his 'minion.' They capture Gaveston and put him to death, but the king at once takes new favourites, the Spensers, and goes to war with the barons to revenge Gaveston. The nobles are defeated, several of them put to death and Mortimer imprisoned in the Tower. Meanwhile, the Queen, who has been sent to France to negotiate terms, has raised an army and, joined by Mortimer, invades England. The king is defeated. He takes refuge in Neath Abbey, where he is seized, and taken to Kenilworth and forced to abdicate in favour of his son. He passes through the hands of a series of keepers, who prove too merciful, since Mortimer, now Lord Protector, is seeking to destroy him by various kinds of ill-treatment. When this does not have the desired effect, Lightborn is sent to murder him in a way that shall show no bodily injury. The murderer is discovered and the young king, Edward III, executes Mortimer and sends his mother to the Tower for complicity.

In founding his play on Holinshed, Marlowe gave far more importance to Gaveston than his source does, making Gaveston's five years (1307–1312) as the king's favourite the centre of the first half of the action. The second half, after Gaveston's death, covers the period from 1312 to 1330. With the events of a whole reign thus telescoped, Marlowe scarcely had the opportunity for either lyrical flights or any extended development of character, even if his talent had lain in that direction. The style is therefore in the main subordinated to the action. The swift cut and thrust of the dialogue matches the banishing, the recalling, the threatening and the fighting of which the play mostly consists. This has rather a confusing effect, and the editors of the latest edition remark that 'the dramatist sometimes seems like a man trying to tie up a parcel in a piece of paper too small for it.'

Nevertheless, *Edward the Second* is remarkable in its time for its firmness of structure and the ruthless energy of its development. The adaptation of Holinshed with an eye to dramatic effect also shows considerable skill. Marlowe may have learnt something from Shakespeare in this regard, if he worked with him on the *Henry VI* plays. Charlton and Waller think that he was drawn to the subject 'by the pathos and horror of Edward's end.' True, the play gave him an opportunity to exhibit cruelty in a most excruciating form; but he was equally drawn to it by his own homosexual leanings—by Edward's infatuation with Gaveston, since he makes this the centre of the play. It is noticeable, too, that, unlike Holinshed's Edward II, Marlowe's king never admits to being in the wrong. He remains wilful and defiant to the last, frustrated rather than defeated. Even at the end, after he has been standing for a week in all the filth of the castle sewer, he recalls his days of chivalry and tells Lightborn to remember that he is still a king. In such scenes Marlowe has come a long way from his belief that 'a god is not so glorious as a king.' In *Edward the Second* he sets out deliberately to destroy his earlier ideal of kingship.

Apart from Gaveston, Mortimer is the next most important figure in the play. Mortimer, in his dissimulation as Lord Protector, closely follows the precepts of Machiavelli. He takes pride in being more feared than loved, but when he can win his ends by smooth words he does so. Though he finally murders the king, he had earlier told the barons that, however they bore it out, it was treason to be up against the crown. 'It is a special point of Government,' wrote Machiavelli, 'to win men with smooth words, or roundly to cut them off.' Mortimer's mistake was not to 'cut off' the king's son, an oversight which cost him his life.

Like all Marlowe's women, Isabel is colourless; her continuing love for the king is the most touching thing about her. After she has procured Gaveston's recall, Edward, somewhat ironically, hangs a golden tongue round her neck because she can plead so well. Kissing him, she cries:

> nor let me have more wealth,
> Than I may fetch from this rich treasury:
> O how a kiss revives poor Isabel!

The conceit anticipates, or echoes, *Venus and Adonis*— 'And suck his lips' rich treasury dry.' But poor Isabel, indeed! Her implacable cruelty to the king towards the end of the play is understandable enough after his treatment of her. Marlowe always brings Isabel on to the stage just at the moment when her appearance is least welcome to Edward—at the height of one of his transports with Gaveston. From his point of view, it is natural that he should turn away from her in aversion; one is only puzzled at the simple-mindedness of her own behaviour, especially as she tells Mortimer

> For never doted Jove on Ganymede
> So much as he on cursed Gaveston.

Gaveston, indeed, with 'his sensual and luxuriant imagination, his devil-may-care insolence, his ironical recklessness,' may, suggest Charlton and Waller, 'be very much what Marlowe himself actually was.' Certainly his replies to the three poor men who seek his patronage in the first scene of the play have much of Marlowe's inhuman logic and pride, while his great soliloquy in the same scene glows with the very spirit of the Italian Renaissance.

> Sometime a lovely boy in Dian's shape,
> With hair that gilds the water as it glides,
> Crownets of pearl about his naked arms,
> And in his sportful hands an olive tree,
> To hide those parts which men delight to see,
> Shall bathe him in a spring, and there hard by,
> One like Actæon peeping through a grove,
> Shall by the angry goddess be transform'd,
> And running in the likeness of an hart,
> By yelping hounds pull'd down, and seem to die. . . .

Gaveston evidently knew only too well what would please the king. The revelant passage in Holinshed is an example of what Marlowe made of his source. Gaveston, writes the chronicler, furnished the court with 'companies of jesters, ruffians, flattering parasites, musicians and other vile and naughty ribalds, that the king might spend both days and nights in jesting, playing, banqueting, and in such other filthy and dishonourable exercises.' This is a far cry from the fine voluptuousness of Marlowe's lines. In its tone of angry moral censure

can be heard an anticipation of the closing of the theatres
by the Puritans. But it was in such pleasures that
Marlowe himself delighted:

> And in the day when he shall walk abroad,
> Like sylvan nymphs my pages shall be clàd;
> My men like satyrs grazing on the lawns,
> Shall with their goat-feet dance an antic hay.

The trouble was, Edward did not know where to
stop. With no sense of reality at all, he was himself
not much more than a player king and life for him was
hardly more than a masquerade. As one of the barons
remarks bitterly:

> When wert thou in the field with banner spread?
> But once, and then thy soldiers march'd like players,
> With garish robes, not armour, and thyself
> Bedaub'd with gold, rode laughing at the rest,
> Nodding and shaking of thy spangled crest,
> Where women's favours hung like labels down.

Indeed, all through the play the barons lecture the king
with the unconcealed contempt that such hunting and
fighting gentry would naturally feel for one of his disposition. Marlowe's attitude to him is ambiguous.
Having built up his actions into a climax of folly and
hysteria during the first half of the play, in the second
half he begins to pity him as a weak, old and helpless
creature at bay—although, it must be confessed, it
comes as something of a shock to find the king suddenly
referred to as 'old Edward' when one had come to
regard him as young and frivolous. But this is the penalty
Marlowe paid for trying to cram so much history into
so short a space. But, of course, if the audience could
be brought to pity the foolish king then the spectacle
of his final sufferings would be all the more terrible.

Marlowe's anti-clericalism breaks out when Edward and Gaveston assault the Bishop of Coventry like a pair of badly behaved schoolboys. It breaks out again when the Archbishop of Canterbury, at the head of a solemn conclave of barons, re-enacts Gaveston's banishment and demands that the king sign the order:

> Why should a king be subject to a priest?
> Proud Rome, that hatchest such imperial grooms,
> For these thy superstitious taper-lights,
> Wherewith thy anti-Christian churches blaze,
> I'll fire thy crazed buildings, and enforce
> The papal towers to kiss the lowly ground. . . .

Marlowe could get away with this sort of thing on the strength of popular anti-papal feeling.

Very splendid is Mortimer's description of Gaveston, but it reflects the manners of Elizabeth's rather than an early fourteenth-century court.

> While soldiers mutiny for want of pay,
> He wears a lord's revenue on his back,
> And Midas-like he jets it in the court,
> With base outlandish scullions at his heels,
> Whose proud fantastic liveries make such show
> As if that Proteus god of shapes appear'd.
> I have not seen a dapper jack so brisk,
> He wears a short Italian hooded cloak,
> Larded with pearl, and in his Tuscan cap
> A jewel of more value than the crown. . . .

Ralegh, it will be remembered, was reputed to wear jewels in his shoes alone to the value of 6,600 gold pieces at a time when, as Strype tells us, 'sturdy beggars were strung up apace,' many of whom were soldiers broken in the wars. Though bitterly resenting his influence with the king, what the barons really object to about Gaveston is his free and unlimited access to the treasury. For when the Elder Mortimer magnanimously reminds the others that not only 'the mightiest kings have had their minions,' but also 'the wisest men,' Tully and Socrates, his nephew replies that it is not 'the king's wanton humour' that grieves him so much as the fact that the country's money is being wasted. But when the king tells the nobles to prepare for a tournament to celebrate his niece's marriage to Gaveston, the devices with which they emblazon their shields turn out to be ironical comments on his relationship with his favourite. 'Base leaden earls that glory in your birth,' is Gaveston's riposte. 'Go sit at home and eat your tenants' beef'—the implication being that they are simply bores, out of place among men of sensibility.

From the moment when Edward is defeated and seeks sanctuary in Neath Abbey, Marlowe gives him some of his most beautiful lines:

> But what are kings, when regiment is gone,
> But perfect shadows in a sunshine day?

Edward has lost all his friends one after the other—Gaveston, the Spencers, Baldock; and through 'the reluctant pangs of abdicating royalty' a new, silver-sweet music begins to sound, in the king's invocation of the heavenly bodies, which anticipates the last great soliloquy of Faustus:

> Continue ever thou celestial sun,
> Let never silent night possess this clime,
> Stand still you watches of the element,
> All times and seasons rest you at a stay,
> That Edward may be still fair England's king.

That he is not still fair England's king he has only him-self to blame, for he had proclaimed earlier that rather than give up his favourites he would 'Make all England's towns huge heaps of stones. . . .' Such a man was clearly unfit to rule, and his tragedy is that he is placed in a position of supreme authority. With a little tact, he could, like James I, have kept both his throne and his favourites.

The character of Lightborn, who takes such a pro-fessional pride in his vocation as murderer, is Marlowe's invention. He is so real that he surely must have been founded upon one of the poet's secret service acquain-tances. He is a very Italianate villain. Mortimer warns him that when he sees the condition of the old king he will begin to pity him. He laughs aside any such suggestion and tells the Protector:

> You shall not need to give instructions,
> 'Tis not the first time I have killed a man:
> I learn'd in Naples how to poison flowers,
> To strangle with a lawn thrust through the throat,
> To pierce the windpipe with a needle's point,
> Or whilst one is asleep, to take a quill
> And blow a little powder in his ears,
> Or open his mouth and pour quicksilver down.
> But yet I have a braver way than these.

—a list of accomplishments appalling in the slick, unemo-tional way they are retailed, and also in the faultless clarity of the verse. It is like looking down into depths of evil which one had expected to be murky, only to be more horrified when they turn out to be crystalline.

The scene of the actual murder is spare and grim. The dialogue which precedes it is laconic and practical, as between practised murderers, not breathless as the exchanges between Macbeth and his wife. Lightborn is giving his instructions to Matrevis and Gurney, the king's keepers.

> Yet be not far off, I shall need your help.
> See that in the next room I have a fire,
> And get me a spit, and let it be red hot.
> *Matrevis* Very well.
> *Gurney* Need you anything besides?
> *Light.* What else? a table and a featherbed.
> *Gurney* That's all?
> *Light.* Ay, ay so when I call you bring it in.

Beyond mentioning the featherbed, the table and redhot spit, Marlowe does not show how 'bravely' Edward was murdered. Its representation would have been too much even for the Elizabethan stage. But it is made all the more repellant by the prolonged ill-treatment that has preceded it—no worse, probably, than that endured by plenty of political prisoners and recusants who fell into the hands of Topcliffe. The almost bored efficiency of Edward's torturers is doubtless based on Marlowe's own experience of how the State broke down the resistance of its prisoners.

The king's cruel, whimpering end is strongly contrasted with the philosophical self-possession of Mortimer when he is led out to execution.

> weep not for Mortimer,
> That scorns the world, and as a traveller,
> Goes to discover countries yet unknown.

—which, in fact, anticipates Hamlet's reflections on death.

In the death scene of Edward, as to an even greater

extent in the final scene of *Doctor Faustus*, Marlowe showed that he had become a master of the classic elements of tragedy—pity and terror. Indeed, the most notable thing about *Edward the Second* is its uncompromising starkness and the severe discipline Marlowe imposed upon his natural lyrical ardour. The emergence of this restraint and the almost cold clarity and precision of the verse, so different from Shakespeare's natural luxuriance, or even from Marlowe's earliest manner, shows that, had he lived and had he been writing for a more scholarly audience, he might, in company with Jonson, have been capable of creating a truly classical English drama.

(vi) THE TRAGICAL HISTORY OF DOCTOR FAUSTUS

Written 1592.

Published. Entered in the Stationers' Register on 7 January 1601 to Thomas Bushell. Earliest known edition is the Quarto of 1604 (A Text), of which one copy survives in the Bodleian Library. Another edition of 1616 (B Text) by Wright differs radically from A Text with the addition of about 550 lines. Of this edition there is a single copy in the British Museum.

Stage history. Probably first performed by Pembroke's company at Court, December 1592, and then at the Theatre the following January, which may be the performance referred to by Thomas Middleton in the *Black Book* (1604). Performed by Admiral's men at the Rose in the autumn of 1594. Under 30 September of that year Henslowe records the receipt 'at docter Fostose' of £3 12s. On 22 November 1602 Henslowe paid, on behalf of the Admiral's company, £4 to William Birde and Samuel Rowley 'for their adicyones [additions] in doctor fostes.'

Source. The History of the damnable life and deserved death of

Doctor John Faustus . . . translated into English by P. F. Gent.,
1592. This was a translation of the German *Historia von D.
Johann Fausten*, Frankfort, 1587. It has been shown that
Marlowe based his play on 'P. F.'s' translation and not on
the original German text.

Plot. Faustus is revealed sitting in his study. He reviews his
studies, rejecting Logic, Medicine, Law and finally Divinity
in favour of Magic. He conjures up Mephostophilis and signs
a pact with Lucifer in his own blood whereby he gives him
his soul in exchange for 24 years during which he is to have
Mephostophilis as his servant and 'to live in all voluptuousness.'
The contradictory promptings of the Good and Evil Angels
symbolize the conflict in Faustus' mind. His desire to repent
of his bond is sharply checked by Lucifer and Belzebub, who
divert him with the spectacle of the Seven Deadly Sins. But
unable to achieve anything very much by his magical powers
and falling into despair at the prospect of hell, Faustus is
about to kill himself, at the prompting of Mephostophilis,
when an Old Man appears and persuades him to pray for God's
mercy. Mephostophilis appears and threatens to tear him
to pieces for going against his bond, whereupon he signs a
second bond with Lucifer. Faustus then asks for Helen of
Troy as his paramour. On the night of the expiration of his
24 years lease of life he awaits the hour of midnight with
increasing terror and despair. As midnight strikes the devils
seize upon him and bear him shrieking to hell.

Such is the main plot. The play, however, is eked out
by a good deal of slapstick comedy in which Wagner, Faustus'
apprentice, parodies his master's conjuring tricks. There are
also scenes of anti-papal foolery at the Vatican and flat,
tedious scenes at the court of the Emperor Charles V.

Doctor Faustus is Marlowe's greatest and most personal
tragedy. To all intents and purposes, he stands before
us on the stage in the person of the German scholar
who was known as 'the insatiable speculator.' The play

is worked out in terms of mediæval theology, which still dominated a large part of Marlowe's mind and imagination. The tragedy turns upon his intellectual rejection of Christianity and his emotional attachment to it. 'Thus,' writes Dr. Kocher, 'the drama is not primarily one of external action but of spiritual combat within the soul of one man, waged according to the laws of the Christian world order.'[1] In the first scenes we witness the temptation to which Faustus is exposed by his intellectual pride, which leads him into a bargain with the devil; in the second half of the play we are shown his agonized struggles to escape damnation. The construction is as simple as a morality, and shows how near the Elizabethans still were to the mediæval world view.

The English Faustbook describes Faustus as 'not unlike that enemy of God and his Christ that for his pride was cast into hell.' In Marlowe's play we read:

> *Faust.* Was not that Lucifer an angel once?
> *Meph.* Yes Faustus, and most dearly lov'd of God.
> *Faust.* How comes it then that he is prince of devils?
> *Meph.* O by aspiring pride and insolence,
> For which God threw him from the face of heaven.

The opposite of intellectual pride is despair, and it is because of his despair that Faustus is damned. Mephostophilis tells him that hell is absence from God, a spiritual condition.

> *Faust.* Where are you damn'd?
> *Meph.* In hell.
> *Faust.* How comes it then that thou art out of hell?
> *Meph.* Why this is hell, nor am I out of it:

[1] Kocher, *Christopher Marlowe*, p. 104.

Think'st thou that I who saw the face of God,
And tasted the eternal joys of heaven,
Am not tormented with ten thousand hells,
In being depriv'd of everlasting bliss?

These are really the most tragic lines in the drama—
the realization of the full significance of this state of
absence from God. It was also Marlowe's own private
hell.

Faustus is shown on the path to damnation in the
opening scenes of the play, when he takes two texts,
from *Romans* and *The First Epistle of St. John*, and com-
bines them into a doctrine of despair whereby man is
inevitably damned for his sinful nature. Kocher has
pointed out that this gloomy Calvinistic doctrine of
predestination entirely leaves out of account the central
teaching of Christianity: the doctrine of grace, which
taught that man is redeemed through the sacrifice of
Christ, if only he will have faith in God's mercy and
repent of his sins. Hence, in the blaze of terror of his
last soliloquy Faustus cries out

See see where Christ's blood streams in the firmament.
One drop would save my soul, half a drop, ah my
Christ!

But by then it is too late. Marlowe was perfectly
aware of this doctrine of grace, but he shows that
Faustus cannot repent because his heart is hardened
with intellectual pride. As a result, he can only see
God as an enemy, as the avenging father-figure. Neither
the Old Man, who makes a final attempt to save Faustus'
soul, nor the Good and Evil Angels are in the English
Faustbook—the one symbolizing the promptings of his
heart, the other of his intellect. The fact that he is not

predestined to damnation is shown by the fact that he
always has the choice of repentance open to him right
up to the last scene.

Such is the theological framework of the drama. But
we can also see it, like Professor Ellis-Fermor, as 'a faithful revelation of a mind in transition between two con-
ceptions of the universe. As Faustus wavers between
his good and evil angels, between God and the devil,
so we may see Marlowe hesitating between the sub-
missive acceptance of a dogmatic system and a pagan
simplicity of outlook to which instinct and temperament
prompted him.'[1] Marlowe's apostasy, according to
this view, lay in his final submission to 'the super-
stitions of his contemporaries.' But this is, perhaps,
to over-simplify, from a twentieth-century rationalistic
standpoint, what was for Marlowe still an agonizing
conflict. Kocher is nearer the truth when he writes
that 'however desperately his desire to be free, he was
bound to Christianity by the surest of chains—hatred
mingled with reluctant longing, and fascination much
akin to fear.'[2]

How much *Doctor Faustus* is really Marlowe's personal
drama can be seen by referring to his original, the Dr.
John Faustus of the Faustbook. This doctor of Divinity
of Heidelburg University, writes Dr. E. M. Butler in
Myth of the Magus, appears to have been a big name in
magic only in his own estimation. 'His silly vauntings
irritated, and sometimes maddened, his learned contemporaries, the humanists; who, being themselves all
more or less absorbed in occult speculations and experi-
ments, knew all his claims were preposterous.' He
declared that Christ's miracles were nothing to his
and called the devil his brother-in-law. In 1532 we

[1] U. M. Ellis-Fermor, *Christopher Marlowe*, p. 67.   [2] Op cit., p. 119.

find him referred to as 'the great sodomite and necro-
mancer,' when the city of Nuremburg refused him a
safe conduct. He played numerous silly and cruel
pranks—faithfully reflected in the fooling of the sub-
plot of Marlowe's play—on others. There could scarcely
be a figure less like Marlowe's conception than the
quack and braggart of reality. The Faustbook itself,
as Dr. Butler shows, is little more than an amalgam of
various magical practices plagiarized from other sources.
Indeed, tales of magic reach their lowest level in the
biography of Faust, though it is here that Mephostophilis
makes his first appearance—he did not become Mephisto-
philes till later.

Marlowe ennobles and spiritualizes the whole conception. In the Faustbook, for instance, after Faustus
has signed his second pact with the devil, Mephostophilis provides him with a whole harem of women
and succubae, 'To the end that this miserable Faustus
might fill the lust of his flesh and live in all manner of
voluptuous pleasures.' Among the succubae was the
spirit belived to be Helen of Troy. The classical gods
and demi-goddesses had become the devils of the
Christian church—hence the force of Faustus' exclama-
tion, as he kisses Helen, 'Her lips suck forth my soul.'
According to Christian doctrine, to have sexual con-
nection with succubae is to be damned. Marlowe's
address to the spirit of Helen, in whom was embodied
for him the lost beauty of the classical world, soars
to a peak of ecstasy. The Faustbook, on the other
hand, merely describes her as 'so beautiful and delightful
a piece, that he could not be one hour from her.'
Following his source, Marlowe makes Faustus' pact
with the devil depend on the doctor being able to 'live
in all voluptuousness.' But this 'insatiable speculator'

is not interested in women—unless they can be made
into sufficiently remote symbols of classical beauty—
except for a brief moment when he tells Mephostophilis that he is 'wanton and lascivious, and cannot live
without a wife.' Mephostophilis replies that 'marriage
is but a ceremonial toy' and produces a devil dressed
as a woman whom Faustus turns from in disgust. What
he is really interested in is discovering the nature of
hell, who made the world, and other astronomical
matters. But above all he desires the supernatural
power which somehow or other is never granted to
him.

As a doctor of divinity, Faustus has already 'with
concise syllogisms Gravell'd the pastors of the German
church' and made 'the flowering pride of the university'
swarm to his problems. Now witchcraft promises
something much more exciting.

> O what a world of profit and delight,
> Of power, of honour, of omnipotence,
> Is promisd to the studious artizan!
> All things that move between the quiet poles
> Shall be at my command: emperors and kings
> Are but obeyed in their several provinces:
> Nor can they raise the wind, or rend the clouds:
> But his dominion that exceeds in this,
> Stretcheth as far as doth the mind of man.
> A sound magician is a demigod.
> Here, Faustus, tire thy brains to gain a deity!

The exultant note of *Tamburlaine* begins to sound once
Faustus decides to match his will with the divine, and
the Evil Angel now tempts him with the thought:'Be
thou on earth as Jove is in the sky.' The possibilities
of magic give rise in his mind to mysteriously beautiful

visions as well as to the more common claims of witch-craft, such as raising storms and drying the sea to recover the treasure of wrecks. Marlowe had evidently read fairly widely in the literature of demonology and witch-craft, but he only instances Roger Bacon, Cornelius Agrippa and Pietro d'Abano of Padua (called in the text Albanus). Like Leonardo and other artists of the Renaissance who were also engineers, he would design 'stranger engines for the brunt of war,' wall all Germany with brass and join Spain to Africa with 'a bridge thorough the moving air.' But nothing comes of all this: even his eager questioning of Mephostophilis results in no more than he knew before. 'Tush,' he exclaims in his university phraseology, 'these are freshmen's suppositions!' Only on the subject of hell does Mephostophilis enlighten him, when he reveals that hell is not only a place of everlasting torment 'within the bowels of the elements,' but a state of mind.

> Hell hath no limits, nor is circumscrib'd
> In one self place, for where we are is hell,
> And where hell is, there must we ever be.

A conception, Kocher points out, which Marlowe could have found in Abelard. Faustus dismisses all this as 'trifles, and mere old wives' tales' and says that he is not afraid of the word damnation

> For he confounds hell in Elysium.
> His ghost be with the old philosophers!

Kyd, it will be remembered, said that Marlowe used to 'gibe at prayers' and 'jest at the divine scriptures'; Gabriel Harvey said that he was a Lucian.

Having achieved so little at the price of his soul, in the second half of the play Faustus begins to waver and bitterly accuses Mephostophilis of depriving him of the everlasting joys of heaven. ''Twas thine own seeking, Faustus,' replies the fiend. 'Thank thyself,' and he proceeds to throw the scholar's humanism back at him with the argument that as heaven was made for man, 'therefore is man more excellent.' 'If it were made for man,' replies Faustus ''twas made for me. I will renounce this magic, and repent.' But the Evil Angel tells him he is a spirit (i.e. a devil) and that God cannot pity him. The powers of evil having reduced him to despair, tempt him to suicide. If he takes his own life, they will have his soul in any case.

So far, Faustus had done nothing with his infernal powers that might not have been accomplished by Merlin or any mediæval enchanter. He has raised the spirits of various classical heroes for Charles V and, like a schoolboy, snatched dishes away from the Pope's table at a feast in the Vatican and smacked His Holiness in the face;[1] he has, we are told, scaled Olympus 'to know the secrets of astronomy' and flown through the air in a chariot drawn by dragons 'to prove cosmography,' his interests being academic to the last.

It is the beauty of Helen of Troy that completes his downfall, for her 'sweet embracings' extinguish in him all desire to repent of his vow to Lucifer. The ecstasy of his address to her is only the prelude to frantic terror and despair, when he realises that his twenty-four years lease of life is up and that nothing now can save him from an eternity of torment. Mar-

---

[1] It is, of course, by no means out of the question that 'these broad and boyish outbreaks of unseemly but undeniable fun,' as Swinburne describes them, are from Marlowe's pen.

lowe excelled in scenes of agony. After the dazzling visions of classical beauty comes the avenging wrath of God, the devils and hell fire of the church. It is nevertheless in the opposition of these two worlds —the classical and the Christian—both of which seemed to have claimed him equally, that Marlowe reached his highest flights as a poet: the final soliloquy of Faustus being the most lyrically intense single passage in the whole range of Elizabethan drama.

As usual, for all its dangerous speculation on a forbidden subject, Marlowe brings his drama to a perfectly orthodox conclusion. The Chorus enters and gravely points the moral: Faustus is damned for his intellectual presumption.

On the last page of a book printed by Vautrollier, an Huguenot bookseller of Blackfriars, a certain J. G. R. has noted down the following story. During a performance of *Doctor Faustus* at Exeter, the players 'discovered one devil too many amongst them; and so after a little pause desired the people to pardon them, they could go no further with this matter; the people also understanding the thing as it was, every man hastened to be first out of doors. The players (as I heard it) contrary to their custom spending the night in reading and in prayer got them out of the town next morning.' At another performance at the Belsavage Inn on Ludgate Hill, the devil is reported to have appeared in person in reply to Faustus' summons—'The truth of which,' writes William Prynne in his *Histriomastix* of 1633, 'I have heard from many now alive, who well remember it, there being some distracted with the fearful sight.' One, or perhaps both, of these experiences may have befallen Alleyn when he was acting the part of Faustus and to ward off further visitations he performed the meritorious action of founding and endowing the School of God's Gift at Dulwich, which subsequently became Dulwich College. Such stories bear witness to the terrifying effect Marlowe's play had upon his contemporaries. But in this terror lay its main attraction.

Chapter Nine

HERO AND LEANDER

Written 1593.

Published. Entered in the Stationers' Register on 28 September, 1593 by John Wolf. The first surviving edition is that of 1598 issued by Edward Blount, who dedicated it to Sir Thomas Walsingham, in memory of Sir Thomas's patronage of the poet. Only one copy of this edition survives and is in the Folger Shakespeare Library, Washington. To 1598 also belongs the edition of Paul Linley, containing Chapman's continuation of the poem. One of this last is in the British Museum.

Sources. The *Hero and Leander* of Musaeus, an Alexandrian poet of the fifth century, probably in the Latin version of F. Paulinus (1587), also Ovid's *Heroides*.

The Fable. Leander, a youth of Abydos, meets Hero in the Temple of Venus, during the Festival of Adonis, where she officiates as a priestess, and they fall in love at first sight. Hero tells Leander that she lives in a tower by the seashore and invites him there at night. The tale of Mercury, Cupid, Jove and the Destinies concludes the first Sestaid as an illustration of why the Fates are evilly disposed towards true lovers and why scholars are poor.

Leander spends the night at Hero's tower and in the morning returns to Abydos. Unable to bear separation from Hero, he jumps into the sea and swims the Hellespont to Sestos. On the way he is carried off to the bottom of the sea by Neptune, who mistakes him for Ganymede. He arrives at Sestos exhausted by this experience. He makes love to Hero. The lovers are interrupted by another dawn.

Like so much of Marlowe's work, *Hero and Leander* is a fragment and stops short after 818 lines, which only carry the story up to the union of the lovers. There is a certain incoherence in the structure of the poem due to its Elizabethan lavishness of descriptive imagery and mythological incident. In this it is as typical of its age as *The Faerie Queene* or the *Arcadia*. Its wit and airy brilliance, and the 'inveigling harmony' of the versification, act upon the mind like an intoxicant.

Marlowe may have begun *Hero and Leander* at Thomas Walsingham's house at Scadbury during the plague, when the theatres were closed in the spring of 1593. If so, it is his last work, interrupted by his death in May of that year. Certainly there is no other work of his in which he is so serene, so at ease with himself. His free handling of the heroic couplet and the Scholastic sophistry of Leander's wooing point forward to Donne rather than back to Spenser. The versification is, in fact, far more modern than Shakespeare's in *Venus and Adonis*, which was probably written about the same time, or perhaps shortly before, being entered in the Stationers' Register on 18 April 1593. Altogether, there is a maturity in *Hero and Leander* which argues powerfully against the theory which would give it to the Cambridge years, although its mood is in some respects a return to the attitude implicit in the Ovid translations. Its verbal parallels with *Dido* can, on the other hand, be accounted for on the supposition that Marlowe took up his earliest tragedy and began to revise it at this time—a hypothesis supported by the maturity of much of its verse. There is, in fact, a reference to *Hero and Leander* in both *Dido* and *Edward the Second*.[1]

---

[1] i.e. in Gaveston's first speech.

The poem opens on to a glittering sunny scene with light flashed off the waves of the Hellespont, and a kind of briny exhilaration runs through it from first to last. Its polished epigrams suggest Pope or Byron rather than Keats. Sly humour is implicit in the description of Hero's ceremonial robes, belonging to her office as 'Venus' nun'—Elizabethan slang for prostitute. Very different in tone is the rapturous description of Leander.

> His body was as straight as Circe's wand,
> Jove might have sipt out nectar from his hand.
> Even as delicious meat is to the taste,
> So was his neck in touching, and surpast
> The white of Pelops' shoulder. I could tell ye,
> How smooth his breast was, and how white his belly,
> And whose immortal fingers did imprint
> That heavenly path, with many a curious dint,
> That runs along his back. . . .
> Some swore he was a maid in man's attire,
> For in his looks were all that men desire. . . .

Burlesque breaks out again in the description of the 'church' of Venus, where Bacchus swings like a monkey from the ceiling by one hand, while with the other he crushes out the juice of sea-green agate grapes into his mouth. Through the crystal pavement may be seen representations of the less respectable exploits of the Olympian gods.

Hero is described to perfection in one line—'Hero so young, so gentle, and so debonair.' The meeting of the lovers anticipates the meeting of Romeo and Juliet at Capulet's feast, with its gravely beautiful lines:

> These lovers parled by the touch of hands:
> True love is mute, and oft amazed stands.

Yet Marlowe seasons his romantic story of young love with a detached and cynical wit, which glitters in his lines like a fine deposit of salt. Leander's verbal siege of Hero's virginity is echoed both in its dialectic and its phase-facility by Shakespeare's *Sonnets*:

> One is no number, maids are nothing then,
> Without the sweet society of men.

Marlowe's arguments are wittier and more scholastic and less purely conceited that Shakespeare's. Of virginity Leander tells Hero:

> Of that which hath no being do not boast,
> Things that are not at all are never lost.

As a priestess of Venus, he adds slyly, she is committing sacrilege by refusing Venus' rites and 'thee as a holy idiot doth she scorn.' When, however, his eloquence has had the desired effect and Hero surrenders herself, Leander is not quite sure what is expected of him. Here Marlowe anticipates the very accent of Byron's *Don Juan*.

> Albeit Leander rude in love, and raw,
> Long dallying with Hero, nothing saw
> That might delight him more, yet he suspected
> Some amorous rites or other were neglected.

Such half-knowledge is a condition of adolescence. How beautiful is the setting Marlowe provides for their love in Hero's tower –

> Far from the town (where all is whist and still,
> Save that the sea playing on yellow sand,
> Sends forth a rattling murmur to the land,
> Whose sound allures the golden Morpheus
> In silence of the night to visit us.)

Hero is so gentle that even Cupid grieves to see her struck with his burning shaft.

> And as she wept, her tears to pearl he turn'd,
> And wound them on his arm, and for her mourn'd.

A long digression, explaining why the Fates hate lovers and why scholars are always poor, interrupts this pretty love story with an air of personal grievance.

> And few great lords in virtuous deeds shall joy,
> But be surpris'd with every garish toy;
> And still enrich the lofty servile clown,
> Who with encroaching guile keeps learning down.

—which looks as though Marlowe had been disappointed of the patronage of the great. Possibly noblemen felt that his reputation was too dangerous. But was he, in fact, the rival poet of Shakespeare's Sonnets who sought to win the favour of the Earl of Southampton—or, rather, had he won it at one time and then lost it again, through the rashness of his disposition, to Shakespeare that 'lofty servile clown'? His claims to being this rival poet are in some ways better than Chapman's, especially when Shakespeare accuses his rival of a tongue that made 'lascivious comments in thy sport,' which does not sound like Chapman, but very like Marlowe for whom 'it was meat and drink when he was mocking another man.'[1] There is also a reference in this digression to 'fruitful wits' being driven abroad, from lack of patronage and opportunity at home.

Leander's feeling of loss and his feverish emotional state in his absence from Hero is a condition which

[1] Thomas Lodge, *Wit's Misery*, the character of Derison. See also Lawrence Durrell's letter in *The Times Literary Supplement*, 5 January 1951.

every lover will recognize as being summed up to perfection in the lines

> he seem'd not to be there,
> But like exiled air thrust from his sphere

unless the 'air' should really be 'heir,' which unfortunately spoils the effect. His union with his mistress
is, however, delayed by Neptune, who takes him for
Ganymede as he swims the Hellespont—another diver-
sion introduced into the poem by Marlowe—and carries
him off to the depth of the sea, where

> in low coral groves
> Sweet singing mermaids sported with their loves.

Neptune realises his mistake when Leander begins to
choke and there is a queer account of the aquatic sports
which follow while 'the sapphire visag'd god' frolics
round the harassed lover as he does his best to swim to
Sestos. 'You are deceiv'd,' Leander tells him, 'I am
no woman, I.' One cannot help wondering how many
times Marlowe had the same thing said to him by some
equally harassed young player.

When Leander finally reaches Hero's tower we reach
the climax of the poem. The love making, so charmingly
and tenderly described, reveals a side of Marlowe's
nature that is scarcely evident in his plays.

> Love is not full of pity, as men say,
> But deaf and cruel, where he means to prey.
> Even as a bird, which in our hands we wring,
> Forth plungeth, and oft flutters with her wing,
> She trembling strove; this strife of hers (like that
> Which made the world) another world begat
> Of unknown joy. Treason was in her thought,
> And cunningly to yield herself she sought.

Compared with *Venus and Adonis*, Marlowe's poem is almost empty of sensual feeling. Marlowe's woman is rather that of Botticelli in his *Birth of Venus*, with its delicately crisped sea-waves and the girlish Aphrodite riding on her scallop shell, than Shakespeare's glowing Rubens. Both poets introduce the image of the impatient stallion, though it is Shakespeare's lustful Venus who urges the reluctant Adonis to follow the example of his own horse. *Venus and Adonis* is, however, much more carefully worked out and finished off than *Hero and Leander*, which bears all those marks of haste and ardour characteristic of Marlowe. In fact, this hasty, unsystematic way of working is so characteristic of him, that one wonders how much the fragmentariness of his plays is really due to corrupt texts and the accidents of time.

Edward Blount the bookseller, who published *Hero and Leander*, dedicated it to Sir Thomas Walsingham with an affectionate remembrance of his friend, which should be set beside the character given by Kyd and Baines. 'Sir,' he wrote, 'we think not ourselves discharged of the duty we owe to our friend when we have brought the breathless body to the earth; for albeit the eye there taketh his ever farewell of that beloved object, yet the impression of the man, that hath been dear to us, living an after life in our memory, there putteth us in mind of further obsequies due unto the deceased. And namely of the performance of whatsoever we may judge shall make to his living credit, and to the effecting of his determinations prevented by the stroke of death. By these meditations (as by an intellectual will) I suppose myself executor to the unhappily deceased author of this poem, upon whom knowing that in his lifetime you bestowed many kind favours, entertaining the parts of reckoning and worth which you found in him, with good countenance and liberal affection: I cannot but see so far into the will of him dead, that whatsoever issue of his brain should chance to come abroad, that the first breath it should take might be the gentle air of your liking: for since his self had been accustomed thereunto, it would prove more agreeable and thriving to his right children, than any other foster countenance whatsoever.'

Chapter Ten

MARLOWE AS A DRAMATIST

MARLOWE'S approach to the drama was, at first, primarily that of a lyrical poet, and in *Tamburlaine* he reached at once a pitch of intensity that could not possibly be sustained. After *Tamburlaine* the great lyrical passages are only intermittent, and are subordinated to a growing skill as a dramatist. In *The Jew of Malta*, for instance, after the first act the poet practically disappears and the dramatist takes charge. As we have seen, Marlowe began the play at too high a pitch; he then became interested in the plot for its own sake, and worked it out in the satirical frame of mind which seems to have been the counterpart to his idealism. Unlike Shakespeare, but like Shaw, he was interested in his characters in so far as they embodied ideas. Even in a straight chronicle play like *The Massacre at Paris*, he has to turn aside from the action to allow the Duke of Guise to argue with Ramus about Aristotle. It was not till the end of his life (though he was only twenty-nine when he died) that Marlowe achieved in some passages of *Doctor Faustus* a synthesis of poetry and action. But here, once again, the inspiration is not sustained: the play is botched with long stretches of pedestrian versifying and much primitive foolery, though it concludes with an outburst of sublime poetry—a scene which made an indelible impression on John Donne, for there are several references to it in his sermons.

The rapid passages of dialogue between Faustus and Mephostophilis are indications of what Marlowe might have become as a dramatist had he lived. As Goethe remarked, *Doctor Faustus* is greatly planned; unfortunately the plan is only half carried out.

Formally, *Edward the Second*, which probably belongs to the same year as *Doctor Faustus*, is the most perfect and complete of the plays. To write it, Marlowe evidently subjected himself to a severe discipline, for it is economical, firmly knit, with distinct and credible characters. But compared to *Richard II*, which was partly modelled on it, the play somehow remains, in spite of splendid passages, a cold, neutral-coloured, unsympathetic work, born of the brain rather than of the whole man. Shakespeare's play is in some ways inferior to Marlowe's, but it has the freshness and exuberance of the earth in spring, and Richard himself is a preliminary sketch for Hamlet. Above all, Shakespeare's has a warm and inclusive humanity —the very quality which Marlowe's play lacks, for all its conflict of passionate wills and temperaments. Consequently *Richard II* still holds the stage and *Edward the Second* is never performed in our commercial theatres. The public will put up with Shakespeare's poetry for the sake of his fun, his bawdiness, his sweetness and tenderness, the grandeur and the subtlety of his sense of character; but it will not put up with the unrelieved rhetoric of *Tamburlaine*, or the savage fun of *The Jew*, or the cold ruthlessness of *Edward the Second*, with its horrible ending. *Richard III* was Shakespeare's one experiment in Marlowe's manner.

When all allowances have been made for corruption of texts, the plain fact seems to be that Marlowe, in general, had little interest in building up the successive stages of a five-act drama. With him the initial idea seems to have been everything, that and the end. Delighting in extremes of emotion, he was unequal to the more humdrum tasks of a working dramatist, whose material is not only fire and air, but the common clay of human nature. To some extent the Elizabethan habit of collaboration encouraged this fragmentary approach to the drama.

Recent attempts have been made to trace a coherent plan through the two parts of *Tamburlaine*. But, in reality, there is only what Swinburne calls 'the stormy monotony of Titanic truculence which blusters like a simoon through the noisy course of its ten fierce acts'—only the mounting enormity of the Scythian's cruelties and presumption, punished at last as in a mediæval morality. *Edward the Second* and *Doctor Faustus* are almost equally simple in their design: as Mortimer rises on Fortune's wheel, Edward sinks, and when Mortimer has reached the topmost pinnacle of power, he too 'tumbles headlong down.' The opening Chorus of *Doctor Faustus* compares the doctor to Icarus—'His waxen wings did mount above his reach'—a remarkable piece of self-criticism.

Why, then, it may be asked, do we continue to study Marlowe as a dramatist instead of reading him simply for the poetry in his plays? It used to be said (it was said by Swinburne) that Marlowe was the father of English tragedy and the creator of dramatic blank verse. But Kyd has an equal, if not prior, claim to both titles. Certainly Marlowe is the greatest poet working in the drama before Shakespeare, and perhaps, to quote Swinburne again, 'the first English poet whose powers can be called sublime.' He it was who brought dramatic blank verse to life by investing it with a splendour and a quality of soaring aspiration that dazzled his audiences with a sense of the infinite possibilities in man's nature. He set the fashion of the Superman on the Elizabethan stage which inevitably brought to an end the vogue of the children's companies, with their graceful comedies by Lyly, Peele and Greene. After *Tamburlaine*, Greene and Peele became Marlowe's disciples, with disastrous results, as in *Alphonsus* and *Edward I*. Shakespeare, too, fell under his influence for a time, as we have seen, in *Richard III*—with the difference that Shakespeare saw Richard as a pathological case—though it is from the semi-divine stock of Tamburlaine that Caesar, Antony and Othello derive. Perhaps Marlowe's greatest single contribution to the drama was his development of the dramatic monologue, in which the stiff line unit of Peele and Kyd takes wing, wheeling and soaring in an eagle flight of lyrical paragraphs, which are in themselves an expression of the heroic will, demanding a conception of drama far above 'the jigging veins of rhyming mother wits.'

But this is only how Marlowe began. By the time he came to write *The Jew of Malta*, *Edward the Second* and *Doctor Faustus*, his verse had divested itself of its jewel-encrusted singing robes and become a very much more flexible instrument. In the same way, he moved from the barbaric splendours of Tamburlaine, where whole scenes are devoted to the description of armies and their equipment, to the sophisticated feeling for beauty of Gaveston's opening soliloquy in *Edward the Second*, and the exalted rapture of Faustus's address to Helen. In Faustus's last soliloquy, Marlowe breaks the tyranny of the decasyllabic line altogether and anticipates, in the freedom of its movement, the verse of Shakespeare's last period.

Marlowe differed from the other University Wits

by the energy and precision of his mind. Elizabeth
Holmes has pointed out that he makes frequent use of
such verbs as 'shatter,' 'dance,' 'shiver,' 'prancing,'
'dancing', 'leap,' and 'tilt' to express the force and
resilience of his imagination. 'And in the frequent
descriptions of countless hosts and far-reaching spaces
we see him emphasizing number and measure only to
suggest the infinite; so that the thickly scattered place-
names and adjectives, and even Tamburlaine's boasting,
take on a metaphorical, metaphysical tone in this
stretching towards infinity.'[1] And she goes on to define
'a metaphysical quality in imagination, not shaped in
thought, but sometimes latent in the atmosphere of his
work. . . . But Marlowe, with his explorer's ambition,
and his triple intensity of sense and brain and spirit,
had not time to finish the discoveries he began.' Rupert
Brooke sums up the difference between Marlowe and
Kyd when he compares Kyd's contribution to a flaming
torch carried into a dark theatre, and Marlowe's to
the opening of a thousand doors and the flooding of
everything with sunlight. This flaring, smoky light is
indeed characteristic of *The Spanish Tragedy*, so melo-
dramatic, so lurid. The opening of the second act of
The Jew of Malta shows the influence of Kyd's favourite
imagery of darkness and night, and there are echoes of
it in *The Massacre at Paris*. With his taste for the sinister,
Marlowe was by no means all sunlight. His true disciple
in the drama is Webster—master of subtle and Italianate
evil.

The greatest influence of Italy upon Marlowe came
through Bruno and Machiavelli. He caught the Nolan's
sense of infinity and, with the realism which marks
every genuine poet, recognized that the Florentine

[1] *Aspects of Elizabethan Imagery*, pp. 19–24.

had correctly diagnosed the nature of political man. Caesar Borgia was for Machiavelli a supreme example of political acumen, and with his 'Aut Caesar, aut nihil' he might have been one of Marlowe's heroes himself.

Much has been written to show that Marlowe collaborated with Shakespeare in the Henry VI plays in what used to be regarded as their earlier forms, *The First Part of the Contention* and *The True Tragedy of Richard Duke of York*. But it now seems likely that these are only bad quartos of the plays which appear in the Shakespeare Folio as 2 and 3 *Henry VI*. The tendency of modern scholarship is to discredit earlier theories of multiple authorship and to believe that Heminge and Condell knew what they were doing when they included these plays among Shakespeare's works. Nevertheless, the monologues of Richard, Duke of York, in 2 *Henry VI*, have the accent of the Duke of Guise and some lines are written in direct imitation of Marlowe

> And therefore I will take the Nevils' parts,
> And make a show of love to proud Duke Humphrey,
> And, when I spy advantage, claim the crown,
> For that's the golden mark I seek to hit:
> Nor shall proud Lancaster usurp my right,
> Nor hold the sceptre in his childish fist,
> Nor wear the diadem upon his head,
> Whose church-like humours fits not for a crown.
>
> Act I. sc. i.

And when Cardinal Beaufort says:

> That he should die is worthy policy;
> But yet we want a colour for his death:
> 'Tis meet he be condemn'd by course of law.
>
> Act. III. sc. i.

Barabas might be speaking. Moreover, in contrast to
the confusion of style evident in the two other parts of
Henry VI, the second part is consistent in tone, and this
tone is one we associate with Marlowe—cold clarity
of intellect and a corresponding lack of human feeling.
Richard Plantagenet is not only a Machiavel, he has
the special brand of grim humour of Marlowe's heroes:

> Fie—charity for shame! speak not in spite,
> For you shall sup with Jesu Christ to-night.

But this is no more than to show how much Shakespeare
was under Marlowe's influence at this time, and instead
of attempting to trace the hands of Greene, Peele and
others in these plays, we should recognize that Shakespeare
was simply making use of the dramatic idiom of his
age. It was from 3 *Henry VI* that Greene, in his *Groatsworth of Wit*, took the unfortunate line 'O tiger's heart
wrapt in a woman's hide' and parodied it as an example
of what happens when common players like Shakespeare
attempt to write blank verse in imitation of their betters.
But Greene, had his purpose been other than to sneer
at Shakespeare, could have chosen lines more vivid,
passionate and dramatic than he, or even Marlowe,
could have ever compassed. The Henry VI trilogy,
indeed, shows in spite of crudities a graver, more responsible spirit and a greater sense of historical destiny than
appears in any work of Marlowe's. Already in these
early plays Shakespeare gives evidence of a constructive
power beyond that of any of his contemporaries, and
their unity of purpose and design becomes increasingly
apparent the more they are studied.[1]

J. M. Robertson, disintegrator-in-chief, not content
with tracing Marlowe's hand in the Henry VI trilogy,

[1] E. M. W. Tillyard, *Shakespeare's History Plays*.

would credit him with considerable portions of *Titus Andronicus*, *The Taming of the Shrew* (in an earlier version), *Richard III*, *The Merchant of Venice*, *Romeo and Juliet*, *King John* (in an earlier form), *Henry V* (in an intermediate version between *The Famous Victories* and the Folio play) and *Julius Caesar*. He applies the test of style to plays written when Shakespeare was a very chameleon of style. Evidence of Marlowe's hand in *Romeo and Juliet*, for instance, rests on no better evidence than the similarity of such passages as:

> A fair young maid, scarce fourteen years of age,
> The sweetest flower of Citherea's field. . . .
>
> *The Jew of Malta*

and

> Death lies on her like an untimely frost
> Upon the sweetest flower of all the field. . . .
>
> *Romeo and Juliet*

or

> But stay, what star shines yonder in the east?
> The lodestar of my life, if Abigail.
>
> *The Jew of Malta*

and

> But soft! what light through yonder window breaks?
> It is the east, and Juliet is the sun!
>
> *Romeo and Juliet*

The similarity is apparent and we may take into account Marlowe's habit of repeating himself. But, in each case, the original idea is transmuted into a higher order of poetry altogether. Many other examples of such indebtedness can be quoted from Shakespeare's plays, but they only go to show either that the Elizabethans thought nothing of plagiarism, or that Shakespeare, having been struck by certain lines in a very popular play, unconsciously remembered them when he came to write similar scenes himself. In a sense, his greatness lay in this ability to make a synthesis on a higher level of accomplishment of all the elements in the drama of his time.

It is just possible that some of Marlowe's plays have not survived. There was the comedy, *The Maiden's Holiday*, burnt by Warburton's cook; there was the play about Heliogabalus, entered in the Stationers' Register for June 1594 and coupled by Greene in his *Perimedes* with *Tamburlaine*, when he writes of Marlowe 'daring God out of his heaven with the atheist Tamburlan, or blaspheming with the mad Priest of the Sun.' Greene congratulates himself that he, any rate, is not guilty of 'such impious instances of intolerable poetry, such mad and scoffing poets, that have prophetical spirits as bred of Merlin's race.' The enormity of the subject would have appealed to Marlowe. There is also a lost play about Hannibal, which appears to be referred to in the first two lines of the opening chorus of *Doctor Faustus*:

> Not marching now in fields of Thrasimene,
> Where Mars did mate the Carthaginians,
> Nor sporting in the dalliance of love,
> In courts of Kings where state is overturn'd,
> Nor in the pomp of proud audacious deeds,
> Intends our Muse to vaunt his heavenly verse.

Lake Trasimenus was the scene of one of Hannibal's greatest victories in the wars between Carthage and Rome, and the figure of Hannibal would be as likely as Tamburlaine to appeal to Marlowe, especially as he had already written a play on a Carthaginian subject. If both these plays had survived and if they were by

Marlowe, the transition in style from *Tamburlaine* to *The Jew of Malta* might not appear so abrupt.

It is noticeable, however, that for all his reputation for atheism and dangerous thought, Marlowe is always careful to conclude his plays with the most unexceptionable sentiments. This is, of course, only to be expected, as he could have done no less. His popularity was due to the fact that he gauged correctly the taste of his audience, who enjoyed seeing Bajazeth shut up in a cage to starve and invited to eat his wife before she got too thin, and delighted in the devilish ingenuity of Barabas, and shuddered in delicious horror as Faustus conjured up the devil. The stage had to compete in excitement with the bear and bull ring and the public gallows. Dramatists could not afford to be too tame.

Marlowe's plays were performed during his lifetime at the Theatre and probably the Curtain in Shoreditch, where he lived, at the Rose on Bankside and on the temporarily erected stages in the yards of the great inns in London and the provinces. They were also most likely acted at Court during the Christmas revels. *Dido* was acted by the Children of the Chapel Royal. It is a measure of the swiftness with which the Elizabethan drama developed that only about ten years separates *Tamburlaine* from *Julius Caesar* and, more wonderful still, from *Hamlet*. During this time acting progressed from Edward Alleyn's 'great and thundering speech' to Richard Burbage's far more restrained and subtle art. Acting during Marlowe's lifetime was probably still 'the scenical strutting and furious vociferation' which 'flew from all humanity with the Tamerlanes and Tamar-Chams of this late age' stigmatized by Jonson in his conversations with Drummond of Hawthornden. 'What cares these roarers for the name of king?' asks Shakespeare in *The Tempest*, and perhaps he was thinking of the actors of the old school who bellowed their lines like the town-crier in a voice 'to split the ears of the groundlings.'

When Jonson wrote, in the Prologue to *Everyman in his Humour*, that in his play

> Nor creaking throne comes down, the boys to please,
> Nor nimble squib is seen, to make afeard
> The gentlewomen; nor roll'd bullet heard
> To say it thunders . . .

he was thinking of *Doctor Faustus*, where a throne, symbol of the seats of the blessed, was lowered before the eyes of the distracted doctor to remind him of the eternal bliss he had forfeited by his black arts, and where devils come up through trap-doors out of hell, roaring, with squibs in their mouths, as thunder rolled in the tiring-house. Marlowe made liberal provision for such scenic effects. He was a pioneer in the use of the trap-door in both *The Jew of Malta* and *Doctor Faustus*. An analysis of his stagecraft shows that he made constant use of all the areas of action provided by the Elizabethan stage, which, as Mr. Ronald Watkins has recently emphasized in his book *On Producing Shakespeare*, lent itself much better than the more limited modern picture stage to the continuous action of the Elizabethan drama.

Clowns were a necessity of that drama. Though Marlowe refers scornfully, in the Prologue to *Tamburlaine*, to 'such conceits as clownage keeps in pay,' we cannot be sure that he was not responsible for the more puerile humour of *Doctor Faustus*. It was the printer of the 1590 edition of *Tamburlaine* who 'purposely omitted and left out some fond and frivolous gestures, digressing and in my poor opinion far unmeet for the matter.' He did this presumably without consulting Marlowe, who, unlike Webster, never prepared an edition of any of his plays for the press.

Short as it is, we know more about Marlowe's life than we do about Shakespeare's, though the imagery of a man's poetry will often tell us more of his essential nature than the bare facts recorded in academic and legal documents. But we do know that when Marlowe was eagerly studying the volumes in Archbishop Parker's library at Corpus in 1582, Shakespeare applied for a licence to marry Anne Whateley of Temple Grafton and was, it seems, forced to marry Anne Hathaway of Stratford, a woman eight years his senior whom he had got with child.[1] Shakespeare, we know, was a handsome, well-shaped youth of a very ready and pleasant wit, and perhaps as Stephen Dedalus surmises, the second Anne had played a Warwickshire version of the part of Venus to his Adonis. Shakespeare's imagery shows him to have had both feet firmly planted on the ground, for by far the largest group derives from domestic and country life. With Marlowe, on the other hand, imagery drawn from scholarship and classical literature supplies the largest group. By applying the same card-index methods to Marlowe's poetry as Caroline Spurgeon applied to Shakespeare's, Marion B. Smith has shown that the pattern of his thought is determined by a preoccupation with fire, the flight of birds, the stars, and all things clear, brilliant, swiftly moving and aspiring. Marlowe, indeed, seems to have intellectualized his passions to such an extent that they took the form of a thirst for the remote and the impossible—that *soif de l'impossible* so characteristic

[1] Ivor Brown, *Shakespeare*, pp. 49–55.

of romanticism. But his frustrated earthly nature took its revenge on him in obsessive images of cruelty, in the 'hideous lust of pain' which Swinburne found predominant in Webster, and in what Mario Praz has called his Ganymede complex. 'That like I best which flies beyond my reach,' cries the Duke of Guise in *The Massacre at Paris*, 'Though my downfall be the deepest hell!' Marlowe was a subjective writer who put much of himself into his heroes, and these lines are more appropriate to him than to the Guise. He began works on a great design which he could not complete. Intoxicated by the celestial vistas opened by the 'new philosophy,' he attempted more than he, or anyone else, could achieve. Hence, the fragmentary, passionately intense, nature of his work, and the isolated scenes of unsurpassed lyricism, which he lacked the architectonic power to build into the great structures conceived by his imagination.

SELECT BIBLIOGRAPHY

Brooke, C. F. Tucker, THE WORKS OF CHRISTOPHER MARLOWE (1910); THE REPUTATION OF CHRISTOPHER MARLOWE (1922); THE LIFE OF CHRISTOPHER MARLOWE (see Case, R. H.).

Case, R. H., General Editor THE WORKS AND LIFE OF CHRISTOPHER MARLOWE (1930–33).

Greg, W. W., MARLOWE'S DOCTOR FAUSTUS (1604–1616), *parallel texts* (1950).

Adams, J. Q., SHAKESPEAREAN PLAYHOUSES (1917); MASSACRE AT PARIS LEAF, *The Library*, XIV (1934).

Bakeless, John, THE TRAGICALL HISTORY OF CHRISTOPHER MARLOWE, 2 vols. (Cambridge, Massachusetts, 1942).

Battenhouse, Roy, MARLOWE'S TAMBURLAINE (Nashville, Tennessee, 1941).

Boas, F. S., MARLOWE AND HIS CIRCLE (1929); CHRISTOPHER MARLOWE (1940); DOCTOR FAUSTUS (see Case, R. H.).

Bradbrook, M. C., THEMES AND CONVENTIONS IN ELIZABETHAN TRAGEDY (1935); THE SCHOOL OF NIGHT (1936).

Brent, J., CANTERBURY IN OLDEN TIME (1879).

Bridgewater, John (Aquepontanus), CONCERTATIO ECCLESIAE CATHOLICAE IN ANGLIA ADVERSUS CALVINOPAPISTAS ET PURITANOS (1588).

Brown, Ivor, SHAKESPEARE (1949).

Cellini, Benvenuto, MARLOWE (Rome, 1937).

Chambers, E. K., THE ELIZABETHAN STAGE (1924); WILLIAM SHAKESPEARE (1930).

Charlton, H. B., and Waller, R. D., EDWARD II (see Case, R. H.).

Clark, Eleanor Grace, RALEGH AND MARLOWE (New York, 1941).

Collier, J. P., MEMOIRS OF EDWARD ALLEYN (1841).

Craig, Hardin, MACHIAVELLI'S THE PRINCE: AN ELIZABETHAN TRANSLATION (University of North Carolina, 1947).

Devlin, Christopher, RICHARD TOPCLIFFE, *The Month* (March 1951).

Dick, Oliver Lawson, AUBREY'S BRIEF LIVES (1949).

D.N.B. *s.v.* TOPCLIFFE, GIFFORD, MUNDAY.

Duthie, G. I., THE DRAMATIC STRUCTURE OF MARLOWE'S TAMBURLAINE THE GREAT, PARTS I AND II (*English Studies*, 1948).

Eccles, Mark, CHRISTOPHER MARLOWE IN LONDON (Cambridge, Massachusetts, 1934).

Eliot, T. S., ELIZABETHAN ESSAYS (1934).

Ellis-Fermor, U. M., CHRISTOPHER MARLOWE (1927); TAMBURLAINE THE GREAT (see Case, R. H.).

Greg, W. W., HENSLOWE'S DIARY (1904-8); HENSLOWE PAPERS (1902).

Grosart, A. B., THE LIFE AND WORKS OF ROBERT GREENE (1881-6); THE WORKS OF GABRIEL HARVEY (1884-5).

Hall, E. Vine, TESTAMENTARY PAPERS, III. MARLOWE'S DEATH AT DEPTFORD STRAND (1931).

Harrison, G. B., ELIZABETHAN JOURNAL, 1591-1594.

Harriot, Thomas, A BRIEF AND TRUE REPORT OF THE NEW FOUND LAND OF VIRGINIA (1588); MATHEMATICAL PAPERS (British Museum).

Henderson, Philip, AND MORNING IN HIS EYES: A BOOK ABOUT CHRISTOPHER MARLOWE (1937).

Holinshed, Raphael, CHRONICLES (1578).

Holmes, Elizabeth, ASPECTS OF ELIZABETHAN IMAGERY (1929).

Hotson, Leslie, THE DEATH OF CHRISTOPHER MARLOWE (1926); MARLOWE AMONG THE CHURCHWARDENS, *Atlantic Monthly* (July 1926).

Ingram, J. H., MARLOWE AND HIS ASSOCIATES (1904).

Knox, T. F., THE LETTERS AND MEMORIALS OF WILLIAM, CARDINAL ALLEN, 1532-1594 (1882).

Kocher, H. P., CHRISTOPHER MARLOWE: A STUDY OF HIS THOUGHT, LEARNING, AND CHARACTER (New York, 1946).

Lamb, Harold, TAMERLANE THE EARTH SHAKER (1929).

Latham, Agnes, THE POEMS OF SIR WALTER RALEGH (1951).

Lewis, P. Wyndham, THE LION AND THE FOX: THE ROLE OF THE HERO IN THE PLAYS OF SHAKESPEARE (1927).

McKerrow, R. B., THE WORKS OF THOMAS NASHE (1909).

Mahood, M. M., POETRY AND HUMANISM (1950) (chapter 'Marlowe's Heroes').

Markham, Clements B., NARRATIVE OF THE EMBASSY OF RUY GONZALEZ DE CLAVIJO TO THE COURT OF TIMOUR OF SAMARKAND, A.D. 1403–6 (1859).

Martin, L. C., THE POEMS OF CHRISTOPHER MARLOWE (see Case, R. H.).

Poirier, Michel, CHRISTOPHER MARLOWE (1951).

Praz, Mario, CHRISTOPHER MARLOWE, *English Studies* (Amsterdam, 1931); MACHIAVELLI AND THE ELIZABETHANS, *Proceedings of the British Academy* (March 1928).

Read, Conyers, MR. SECRETARY WALSINGHAM AND THE POLICY OF QUEEN ELIZABETH (1925).

Robertson, J. M., MARLOWE: A CONSPECTUS (1931); ELIZABETHAN LITERATURE (1914).

Seaton, Ethel, MARLOWE'S MAP, *Essays and Studies*, Vol. X (1924); MARLOWE, ROBERT POLEY AND THE TIPPINGS, *Review of English Studies* (July 1929); FRESH SOURCES FOR MARLOWE, *Review of English Studies* (October 1929).

Spurgeon, Caroline, SHAKESPEARE'S IMAGERY (1930).

Stephens, Henry, of Vermont, THOMAS HARRIOT AND HIS ASSOCIATES (1900).

Stowe, John, ANNALS, OR A GENERAL CHRONICLE OF ENGLAND (1592).

Tannenbaum, S. A., THE ASSASSINATION OF CHRISTOPHER MARLOWE (New York 1928).

Walker, Leslie J., THE DISCOURSES OF NICCOLO MACHIAVELLI (1950).

Waugh, Evelyn, EDMUND CAMPION (1935).

Wilson, John Dover, LIFE IN SHAKESPEARE'S ENGLAND (1930).

Yates, Frances A., JOHN FLORIO (1934); A STUDY OF LOVE'S LABOUR'S LOST (1936).

Index